MR PIZZA
AND ALL THAT JAZZ

BY PETER BOIZOT

WRITTEN WITH
MATTHEW REVILLE

2014

D1337485

ISBN (Paperback) 978-0-9930112-2-1
ISBN (Ebook)   978-0-9930112-3-8

Published by Large Things Ltd.

Designed and Set by SWATT Design Ltd www.swatt-design.co.uk

Co-written by Matthew Reville

Printed internationally by Ingram Spark

For more information, or to buy copies of this book
please visit http://www.peterboizot.com/

I would like to thank my friend Matthew Reville for all his hard work putting into writing what has been an incredible life.

It has seen considerable success and embraced great changes as I swept through different stages of my time on the Earth.

I am lucky to have pursued things that were successful.

I am glad those businesses brought me unexpected riches.

I am proud to have invested that fortune back into things I love.

– Peter Boizot MBE

Foreword – Luke Johnson

I consider Peter Boizot to be one of the more remarkable entrepreneurs and philanthropists of our age. So many owe him a debt of gratitude – including me.

Peter introduced decent pizza to the citizens of London in 1965 by opening a restaurant in Wardour Street, Soho. Over the decades, the business he founded – PizzaExpress – has become the most successful British restaurant company ever. Branches are now proliferating all over the world – especially China. It is a dining institution, deeply loved by its customers. I was fortunate enough to take the reins from Peter in the role of Chairman in 1993, and help steer it through one of its greatest periods of expansion. I suspect that without Peter, and his magnificent invention PizzaExpress, my career would have been a great deal less exciting and rewarding.

For almost thirty years, Peter developed and shaped PizzaExpress, combining an outstanding product with stylish surroundings, brilliant economics and ingenious recruitment. Its formula of a simple menu, fair prices, interesting buildings and high service standards was unbeatable. The competition melted away, the legions of fans grew and grew, and for untold thousands PizzaExpress became a byword for an affordable and classy night out.

Meanwhile Peter continued to pursue his other passions such as jazz, hockey, Peterborough, the Liberal Party and St Catharine's College, Cambridge. He also created the Veneziana pizza at PizzaExpress: every one sold has contributed to the Venice in Peril fund. Over £2 million has been raised so far. He has been a magnificent donor to those and other good causes close to his heart, and I think it is true to say that he has given away tens of millions of pounds over the decades.

Peter has also been an extraordinary host, throwing legendary parties at venues like Kettner's and The Great Northern Hotel in his home town, Peterborough. His vast guest lists must have consumed many hundreds of gallons of champagne at Peter's expense, enjoying his munificent hospitality.

The author is at heart a salesman and a dreamer, full of superhuman energy, a bon viveur and a man who is always working on various grand schemes. He has never really received the accolades he deserves for his pioneering work as a popular restaurateur, a charitable giver on a major scale, and someone who has added immeasurably to cultural life in Britain over the last fifty years. I hope this book acts as a reminder to many of all he has achieved.

This autobiography is his astonishing story and I commend it to you.

CONTENTS

INTRODUCTION

"MR BOIZOT, COULD YOU TELL US WHAT A PIZZA IS?"

C an you imagine that question being asked today? It is something that anyone could answer – be they a toddler or a teenager, a parent or a pensioner. The nation's leading brains and biggest dunces would have no problem describing that simple, delightful food.

And yet, when London was in the throes of the swinging '60s, that very question was asked to me by a man whose job was to have his finger on the capital's pulse. It was posed by a distinguished member of the Royal Automobile Club during my nerve-wracking interview to join the capital's most exclusive members' only club.

The year was 1967 – just two years after I had set up the first PizzaExpress, but 20 years after my love for pizza was born during a stint as an au pair in Italy.

The club was based on the forever fashionable Pall Mall. On face value it was a society for motoring enthusiasts, but in reality it was a peacock show: a chance to rub shoulders with the nation's elite. On walking through their luxurious building, you could almost smell the heritage.

It was easy to imagine the Prime Minister meeting the head of the civil service in the opulent Great Gallery, while the biggest celebrities in the world wouldn't look out of place against the art deco chic backing of the

Brooklands Room. The RAC had 106 bedrooms for members to stay in – and every bed was filled nightly by a person worth knowing.

After I was led through that overwhelmingly impressive building to my interview room, I admit I was a little intimidated. I had come from modest, if comfortably middle-class, stock in the charming city of Peterborough. Although I had bluffed conversation with important and powerful people all my life, at this stage I was just a small businessman with a big dream.

But this was not the time to be quaking in your boots. After he asked me to explain what a pizza was, I looked deep into the interviewer's eye and replied, with some gusto, about my love for that gastronomic delight.

I fervently explained how I was first exposed to the dish in its authentic form by the delightful Uzielli di Mari family, who I worked for between finishing school and being conscripted to the army.

I reminisced that I arrived in Italy as a skinny, vegetarian teenager, who chose a dull diet of Heinz baked beans and chips after I shunned my mother's wonderful meat dishes. She was a fine cook, but when the decision was between eating a poor animal's flesh or forsaking her best efforts, I'm afraid the latter won out every time.

But my negative nutrition was forever lost after I became exposed to that most delightful dish – pizza. It opened up a world of culinary opportunity for me. Pizza immediately became a food which was to nurture my body for many years to come. Since finding it I had put on a few healthy pounds to complement my six-foot-one frame.

Now it was my mission to share that splendid food with my fellow countrymen. By the time I had told him my story, I think he wanted to grab a slice himself.

Many have said that my love for pizza is infectious – perhaps that is the secret to my success. My family and friends quite rightly note that I can barely find my way around a kitchen, so I'm no culinary expert. But I know what I like, and I have ample bravado to think others will like it as well.

My enthusiasm won through, and I was offered that much coveted spot in the RAC. I am still a member to this day, and it's just one of a number of things I have to thank pizza for delivering to my life.

PizzaExpress has grown into an international chain, with over 420 restaurants throughout the UK and others as far afield as Hong Kong and India. And yes, it is spelt as one word with no space marks… although most seem to spell it as two words!

Our growth was cemented in Italian culinary tradition – not easy when one is removed from that country by some thousand miles. But we looked to Italy for our initial inspiration, staff members and equipment.

Profits have never been my driving force, but I am lucky to have earned a lot of cash over the years. The money I did earn helped me explore my other great passions. I've never had a business mantra (and never even drew up a single business plan). I simply followed what I am passionate about. If, like me, you are lucky enough to find something you love doing, that is the day you retire from 'work' – or at least its literal definition.

Don't get me wrong, I have put in long hours and tried my utmost throughout my life, but as this book will show,

I have had a hell of a good time doing it. It often hasn't felt like work at all.

But I will get into those things in more detail as the chapters move on. For now, I shall sum things up by saying I am pleased to live in a country today where nobody will ever again have to answer the question, *"What is a pizza?"*.

CHAPTER I:
EARLY LIFE

Quite fittingly, my life reads like a good cook book.

There are nine chapters to my life's story – just like there are nine stages to making the perfect pizza. Those stages of making a pizza share similarities with the stages of my life.

For example, in the 'cook book' of my life, one must consider the formative years that created the building blocks of my character that would guide my choices in adulthood. The first step towards a successful life is making sure your preparation is right. This can come from a number of sources – education, experiences or family.

Similarly, the first step to making the perfect pizza is preparing the ingredients. If the foundations of the dish are not correct, it's impossible for the pizza to come out right. One must not rush to the oven before preparing the ingredients correctly.

1
A (NOT-SO) EXPRESS DELIVERY

I came into the world in an upstairs bedroom on 59 Lincoln Road, Peterborough – then the very last home on the street. The date was November 16, 1929 and I tipped the scales at a mammoth 11 ½ pounds. That must have been one hell of a big push for my dear mother, so if you will excuse the pun I can't have been much of an express delivery.

I was such a big baby that my mother was ill for two months after I was born. There were complications during the birth meaning she was bed-ridden and had to have her appendix removed. Her mum (Granny Culshaw) looked after me while she got back to fitness. In time, she was able to come back to the family home.

I was the first child of Susannah and Gaston Boizot, and they spoilt me rotten. I enjoyed a very comfortable adolescence and never went without. Well, excluding my teenage years of course, when food rations began to be imposed on us all during the Second World War.

My first family home was in Lincoln Road, the main street in the area of Peterborough called New England. It was the heart of the city before later post-war expansions that saw Peterborough replace its vibe of a lovely, large market town for one of an industrial, small city. But I have always loved Peterborough and its people, and despite my international adventures, always kept an anchor in the city.

After my birth, it was not long before I was christened. Photographs do not exist of the day, but I am told it was a packed house in Paston Church for the service by Cannon Lethbridge. I have remained a good Christian in the Church of England for all of my God given 84 years, and the good lord willing I hope to go on serving him for many more years.

My darling mother fed me well, from breast and elsewhere. Despite being a committed vegetarian, I am not ashamed to say she gave me a good portion of raw liver when I was an infant. This was very normal in those days, as it was recommended by the medical profession for iron intake.

We stayed in that house on Lincoln Road until I was two years old, and then the family moved to Stilton, a village famed for its cheese, five miles south of Peterborough. But we didn't last long in the sticks and soon moved back into the city centre, to a brand new house on All Saints Road, a stone's throw from Lincoln Road.

It was a fairly up-market house, but the thing that excited me most about the move was that my grandparents lived just a few minutes' walk away on Harris Street.

They were my mother's parents, and the pair of us would go to see them most days. It was a great thing to have your extended family members so close – and that is something I fear our community lacks these days.

There was also a church on our road, a good bonus for our Christian family. But I believe that was a lucky co-incidence rather than a planned operation. My father went to church regularly, and would take me along every Sunday.

Our new home was called Alberta House. The builder of all the new homes had spent some time in the States,

7

and decided to give American names to all of the houses. It had three bedrooms – a sure sign another would soon join our little brood... and so it was no surprise when my darling little sister, Mary Clementine, was born when I was seven.

The houses were all built in rows back in those days, which gave me plenty of neighbours to befriend – a treat for any small boy. The neighbours were very sociable, and it would actually be a challenge not to make friends.

All the children would play in the streets and in the local parks, which are still there but see much less use from the local youngsters. They seem to stay indoors watching television and playing computer games nowadays, which is a shame. Kids should be active, they should be outdoors exploring.

It was a busy area, and you would bump into many familiar and friendly faces just popping to the nearby shops. There was a Co-Op at the top of the road, handy for picking up sweets, and a wonderful fish-and-chip shop on the nearby Dogsthorpe Road. It was a vibrant, communal place where people would pop in to pick up some grub but stick around to catch up with people from the neighbourhood.

I don't doubt that the friendly spirit of that quaint fish-and-chip shop sowed the seeds for me to push my own restaurants as a social hub later on in life.

2
ALL ABOUT THE BOIZOTS

My wonderful parents, Susannah and Gaston Boizot

A lot of people ask me where the family name 'Boizot' originated from. My father, though raised in England, came from northern French stock. It is a name I am proud of: bold and brash, with a touch of flamboyancy. It has caused many people apprehension as they stumble to work out how to pronounce it. I tell them they should say "Boy-zo", but in reality is should be "Bwa-zzzzz-eau". But that is a bit too much of a tongue twister for the English, so "Boy-zo" it is.

I previously mentioned my sister, and early on in this book I feel I should make a public apology. For three quarters of a century, Mary Clementine Boizot has had to put up with people calling her 'Wendy'. The nickname, which she detests, was one I gave her as a baby and proved harder to shake off than a bulldog with his molars adjusted to the death grip.

I was a fairly precocious child, and took to reading from a very early age. When I was six years old, my mother was due to give birth to her second baby. When my future sister was patiently waiting to be born, her soon-to-be godmother Monica Leverett gave me a copy of J.M. Barrie's book *Peter Pan*.

Monica never had children of her own, but was a maternal figure to hundreds (if not thousands) of children in Peterborough as headmistress of Fulbridge Infants School. Being a wise teacher, she had given me the book because I shared the same Christian name as the main protagonist. With mother and father fawning over the baby bump, what better present to give an attention-hungry child than a book where the swashbuckling hero shares his name?

I became fascinated by the story. As a fellow 'Peter', I fantasised that the book was a description of my own adventures. As I'm sure you are aware, the book's leading lady is Wendy Darling. The name struck a chord with me, and in my fantasy world I needed to find a Wendy to join me on those imaginary adventures to Neverland.

When my sister was born, she was officially registered as Mary Clementine Boizot by our parents. She was named after a family tradition, and became the fourth generation of Clementines from my father's side. However, this heritage didn't cut the mustard with me – who has ever read about the adventures of 'Peter and *Mary Clementine*'?

No, I needed a *Wendy*, and I felt my sister could play that role. I simply refused to call her anything but Wendy, in the hope that she could help me to achieve my rightful position of being the real life Peter Pan.

The nickname caught on fast; everybody called her Wendy. It was taken on by parents, grandparents and family friends and years down the road by teachers and even future generations of Boizot family members.

Sometimes she finds this quite irritating, understandably, and often reminds me that her name is not Wendy but actually Mary Clementine. But to me and most others, she will always be Wendy.

While I do have some apologies to make for naming her after Peter Pan's companion, she does have to count herself lucky that she wasn't born a boy... or else she would have ended up as Captain Hook!

Saying that, maybe I'm also the lucky one not to have a brother. I'm not sure that would have gone down well due to my competitive nature. Having a brother would have meant two boys competing for my mother's attentions, and that just wouldn't do. So, all in all, I was very happy to have a sister.

Most family holidays were to nearby Fenland towns like Snettisham and Hunstanton. They felt terribly exotic at the time, but in hindsight they were very close. However, our money was earmarked for more functional things, and I remember one mooted holiday to Cromer being rejected by my father because it was too posh for us. Such was life.

My father Gaston was born in London but moved as an infant to Peterborough, then in 'Northamptonshire' but since rebranded most likely for marketing purposes to be in 'northern Cambridgeshire'. He was raised there not by his parents, but by his extended family. I never talked to him much about it, but the family was not close to that side of grandparents.

He was a wonderful man. He was better known as 'Gus' to everyone who met him, and people of all ages loved him. He was a charismatic story teller, and would pluck the most fantastic stories out of some creative side of his mind where others just had dormant grey matter.

He would often talk about things like rabbits that disappeared down plug holes in the bath. I didn't appreciate his skills until I got a little older and was able to watch him with my younger sister, and her little friends, who would rush to sit on his knee as he told some far-fetched story about monsters while relaxing in his living room armchair. My mum said he was like the Pied Piper.

My father was a true Peterborian. He was a pupil at the excellent Deacon's School in Peterborough, which is now known as Thomas Deacon Academy. After finishing school at the age of 14 he went straight into the Union Insurance Company on Priestgate, near to the cathedral in the city centre. He was a hardworking man and quite well known all over Peterborough in the 1930s and '40s for buzzing around in his little car to visit people.

He stayed in that job for all of his life, although my mother often said he should quit and become a fiction writer. But he stuck it out and was eventually promoted to the lofty position of insurance inspector. I believe that job treated him well. At school, he was one of the only parents privileged to be their own boss – something that I admired and became my own barometer for professional success.

When I was young, my father's position meant he was more flexible to come and see me when I got in trouble, which was more often than I'd like to remember.

My father took good care of us. He worked hard to make sure our life wasn't, and he put in the long hours to make sure all of us enjoyed a good lifestyle. But with that came strict discipline, which on many occasions fused with my cheeky personality for one hell of a good hiding. I remember many occasions when my father would pile on the blows for an offence I felt to be trivial.

But I know my father meant well. Deep down, he was just trying to teach me a lesson and I did rather egg him on. I have an idea that this sort of treatment would not be allowed today, but I feel the world would be better if a tougher line would be taken.

He used to tell me, "You are as good as anyone else, but no better" – a tremendous mantra to instil upon a young person. It gives them self-confidence but at the same time tells you not to look down your nose on other people.

My mother was absolutely dedicated to her family. She was a full-time housewife, and took care of the washing, shopping, bedtime stories and anything and everything in between. She was a wonderful mother. She was also extremely loyal to her parents, and loved visiting them when we moved down the street in All Saints' Road.

My mother was also a terrific cook, and it would drive anyone who ever sampled one of her meals mad to know how much I shunned her lovely dinners. With vegetarianism came a lot of sacrifices of food that others would tell me was quite delightful. She would compensate by giving me first dibs when she was cooking jam tarts.

That would lead to me gobbling down half-a-dozen of them, annoying my father who felt they got in the way of meals. My meals were restricted, by my own fussiness, to chips, beans and Heinz tomato soup.

After all this fuss, it was quite ironic that food would eventually be the industry that gave me my big break!

3
HOW MEETING 'MONSTERS' CREATED A VEGETARIAN

My earliest memories come from when I was five years old, and embarked upon the family holiday that gave birth to my lifelong vegetarianism.

With the plethora of meat dishes now on sale in the restaurant, it may surprise some meat eaters that the founder of PizzaExpress turned to a life of fruit and veg as a child. But it wouldn't surprise a vegetarian.

Pizzas are the most delectable food for a vegetarian: that combination of dough, tomatoes, cheese, herbs and other ingredients turned into a zesty mix of flavour often denied to the diner who objects to eating meat. It was certainly denied to me during my self-imposed vegetarian childhood.

I gave up eating meat during a family holiday up to Scotland in 1934. The trip was organised just as I had become overwhelmed with terror about a giant I had read about in some piece of fantasy fiction. My mother was worried that the holiday could be ruined by my all-encompassing fear that we might run into this fearsome giant. Ever the pragmatist, she alleviated my panic by telling me that not only had the giant recently died, but we would be able to see his grave while up in the Highlands.

During the long drive up to Scotland in my parents' little Austin 7, my father's wonderful storytelling abilities again came to the fore. He told me that not only would we see the giant's burial place, but we would also see the beasts that he kept as pets. He described them as gargantuan, cloven-hooved creatures that weighed over 80 stone (or about the same as 25 boys my age).

My father said they had white skin with large black blotches, and two huge ears that poked out of their skulls and helped them to hear when a predator was approaching. He said they communicated with each other with deep, guttural roars, which I would be able to hear when we approached them from the safety of our car.

Then my mother told me that the locals had found ingenious ways to snare the beasts into traps, and then after slaying them the animal would be cut up and fed to Scottish villagers. She said I would be able to sample some of it, and that it made me so strong no giant would ever want to come after me. Between them, they certainly painted a scary, if exciting, prospect.

As we trudged up closer to Scotland my father suddenly announced he could see the beasts in the field to our side. I quickly turned to take a look at what it was that they had been talking so fearsomely about...

It was a field full of cows nonchalantly grazing.

Compared to the monstrous ogres I had imagined, these creatures looked like happy, foolish, friendly beings who were content to sit in the grass. They were totally innocent of anything that would make them be referred to as monstrous.

I immediately thought back to my mother's promise of eating the 'beasts', and was repulsed at the idea. Why should this docile animal die just so I could fill my belly?

My mother had been feeding me raw liver as a child, and I thought nothing of it. Food was just something that came from a can. However, I was converted to vegetarianism that moment I realised the food came from inside those Scottish cows. I hated the idea of the animal losing its life, and didn't want all the blood that goes with eating it. Plus the concept of my teeth ripping through their flesh was too much to bear.

It was then and there that I vowed to become a vegetarian, and a childhood diet of Heinz baked beans, chips and more Heinz baked beans ensued. Being a vegetarian back then was a rare thing. My mother might have thought it was just a passing phase, but she always stuck up for my right to choose an anti-meat diet. She would say, "The person who best knows what Peter wants is Peter."

The other children in my class often marvelled at my vegetarianism – I think I was the only one in the school.

I had a lot of fun as a child. One treat bought for me by my parents was a three-wheeled pedal car, ideal for youngsters. I would roam far and wide in it, often near the swimming pool past the wartime tank in the park along Dogsthorpe Road. One time I got a little too near to the water at the duck pond and tanked right into the water.

It took a strong gentleman to rush over and pull me out. As he checked on my condition, I was more worried about my treasured tricycle. Luckily we were both fine, and I pedalled home thinking what a kind man he was.

Cycling was not the only sport I grew a love for. Later would come field hockey, but the joys of team sports were shown to me as a six-year-old boy, when my father took me to my first football match. He was a very keen football man, and supported Leicester City – a professional team 40 miles down the A47.

But, being a Peterborough lad, it was our local team Peterborough United who he took me to see, and I instantly fell in love with the club. We may have not been as illustrious as Leicester, but Peterborough United were the team for me.

The club were affectionately known locally as 'The Posh' – for reasons that do not seem to be universally agreed upon by us fans. Some believe the nickname came after the club was set up in 1921 and new manager Pat Tirrell said he was looking for "Posh players for a Posh team", but I believe that story has been concocted in recent years by people who do not know the true story.

When the club first moved into its London Road stadium in 1934, there was a pub next to the ground called the 'Port Out, Starboard Home', which was known to regulars by the acronym 'POSH'.

Port Out, Starboard Home was first printed on the most expensive tickets of passengers on boats between Britain and India, and that acronym had since been used to denote high-class living. The POSH pub was the place for fans to congregate before and after games (or even during them, if we were on particularly bad form!).

Alcohol became so synonymous with the football experience that fans would say they are going to the POSH instead of watching the match… and the nickname 'Posh' soon became the club's established nickname.

Peterborough United's London Road stadium was a compact ground 15 minutes' walk from my home that was always brimming with atmosphere. I forget my first match, but remember straining in a packed terrace to catch a glimpse of any of the action over a crowded huddle of seemingly impossibly tall fans.

Back in the early days, there were three of us going to Posh games – myself, my father, and my uncle Vic Leverett, who lived in Grantham and was a former footballer himself. Uncle Vic had previously played for Peterborough United, a fact I held with great pride. The standard was not as good as today's team, and they were an amateur side plying their trade in the old Midland League.

The stadium is in the middle of a busy terraced street and that stand caused a whole lot of controversy when it was built. Residents from Glebe Road had been used to peeking into the ground from their street – now this 3,000 capacity stand blocked their view. The stand also caused them problems with their televisions – so it well and truly forced fans out of their homes and into the ground, I suppose.

We always stood on the Glebe Road terrace, behind one of the goals. I used to love going down to the games – with the roaring crowd packed around that magnificent freshly cut green grass. I have been going down to London Road for many years since, and I will never lose my love for Peterborough United.

When I was eight, I also discovered my love of music. My father took me to sing in the ladies' choir at Peterborough Cathedral on Sunday evenings. The cathedral is a gargantuan, wonderful gothic building that looms large over all of Peterborough. It was a privilege to sing there when the city's Christians came to worship.

However, my stint there wasn't without its dramas. I remember one Sunday a monstrous storm hit the city during a service. Rain, thunder and lightning pounded down on the cathedral's high roof – it was almost a Biblical scene.

In the excitement, I fainted right there in the stalls. My father rushed in and carried me to the vestry to recover. Ever the functional pragmatist, he simply dusted me down and sent me back to the service to sing with the ladies.

4
A KING'S EDUCATION

My primary schools were Queen's Drive West and then Saint Mark's School – now known as Gladstone Primary School. From my first day I loved education, but I wasn't one for staying on the right side of the teacher's cane.

I was a cheeky little chap, and during my primary school years I was an apple scrumper – a cardinal sin for any schoolboy. Wherever there was an overhanging apple tree you could expect to see my little legs dangling nearby as I hung from the branches rotting around for some tasty fruit to add to the ration list. I still feel this is a minor slight, but it led me to feel the dreaded sharp side of Ms Harris' and Mr Rowlands' canes numerous of times.

The biggest trouble I ever got into was when, aged 11, I was run over by a car while making my way to class. There were far less on the roads back then, so to be run over was quite an achievement in itself, although my audition to be Peterborough's first piece of human roadkill was anything but planned.

Although Saint Mark's was only a couple of minutes' walk away, I left home already late for the start of the school day and proceeded to hotfoot it to escape another dreaded caning. I steamed across into the busy Lincoln Road and 'pow'... I collided with an oncoming car.

It was totally my fault. I leapt out in front of the vehicle, which was going about 25 miles per hour – certainly fast enough to do some serious damage. It knocked me to the ground, but like any self-respecting 11-year-old, I didn't stay off my feet for long.

Still scared of being late, I quickly gathered my thoughts and, much like when I had fainted in the service during the storm, I leapt back to my feet and ran to my class.

I didn't tell anyone at school – what an embarrassment – but soon my secret was to get out anyway. The head teacher came into my classroom with an anxious-looking gentleman, and said he was looking for the boy he ran over. It hadn't crossed my mind that he was concerned for my health. Seeing the worried look on his face, I made myself known to him (and admitted my foolishness to the class). The man was incredibly relieved, and thankfully the head spared me a caning.

The fact the motorist took time out of his day to check up on me shows just how much people cared back then. I dare say a driver might be tempted not to stop if he hit somebody today, but back in my youth this kind gentleman not only stopped but he tracked down my school and visited each classroom until he found me.

Luckily, I suffered no injuries… although my parents often ribbed me that it left life-long brain damage!

Not long after that incident it was time to move on to a secondary school. My father had heard the prestigious King's School, on nearby Park Road, was offering scholarships for new chorister recruits. This was a fantastic opportunity for him to get me into the best school in Peterborough; all I would have to do is pass the chorister entrance exam and I was in. The one problem – I was still a cantankerous child, so I inevitably didn't want to audition.

The magnificent Peterborough Cathedral

The try-outs were held in Peterborough Cathedral, which was fitting because they were the same illustrious surroundings that the choristers would perform in. My father took me to the gates and explained the importance that I impress the school's admission team with my voice.

My response was to stamp my feet and say I didn't want to sing. When he started to drag me, I grabbed hold of the nearest metal railings with all my might and refused to let go.

It soon became a rather farcical tug of war between my dad and the gates... with me as the ever stretching rope. I'm not sure why I didn't want to audition – maybe it was my way of rejecting growing up (like my namesake and childhood hero Peter Pan). But I clung to those gates for dear life, and was dejected when my father inevitably won the tug of war and dragged me into the cathedral.

Once inside, my demeanour changed. Those grandiose surroundings can clearly inspire even the most raucous of souls, and I decided to give it my best shot, and I sang well enough to be accepted to join the King's School on a full musical scholarship. With hindsight, how grateful I became that my father was stern and forced me inside, as I cannot imagine a finer education than the one that scholarship provided.

My mother always sent me to school looking smart. Soon after starting at King's, she would tell me to wash my neck before leaving the home because otherwise it would look like I came from Boongate – a poorer area of the city. King's School was an exclusive school and she thought it was right to present myself as being worthy of the surroundings.

A sense of professional clothing has continued throughout my life and I always expect a gentleman to at least wear a tie when conducting business matters. I would always wear a full suit – when I'm making a professional proposition, it always helps to 'look the part' to 'be the part'.

At secondary school, my competitive streak started to rub off on academia and I started to get good grades. I did continue to struggle with mathematics though. It was never my strong points – as my accountants over the years could tell you.

Most importantly, I always enjoyed myself. We had classes of about 50, which when you look back on it was an incredibly large number. My two best friends were Dick Taylor and Dick Gray, but there was a large mob of us.

We had good teachers, mainly men, and the facilities were fantastic. The school stayed open even in the harshest of conditions. I remember one winter saw the whole city buried under snow for the best part of three months, but the school stayed open throughout. Living just around the corner, I was there every day, but my swollen class of 50 dropped down to a paltry two for those weeks.

It was just me and my friend Tom Gee, who came in from Thorney on his bike every day – an eight mile cycle that was a fine effort on the best of days, but a monstrous one in the snow.

The biggest social group at the school was us choristers, and I had a great time singing with the school choir. There were two lead singers– Harry Hartley (a tenor) and Stanley Hill (bass). They made an excellent all-embracing duo. There was occasionally Cyril Laxton (alto) and Charles Stimpson (tenor), who filled out the choir. Ray Laxton was another star chorister, and he would eventually go on to be mayor. We had such fun.

Over a sustained period of many weeks, I used a coin to etch my name into one of the arm rest of the pews we sat on in the cathedral. The operation was difficult – I had to avoid the gaze of the dean James Simpson, the bishop or, worst of all, my father. It would have been the thrashing of a lifetime if he saw me doing that, but I got away with it and nobody ever told me off for it.

But I never got caught and it became something of a tradition, with dozens of naughty young boys carving their name into the wood to create an unofficial roster of choristers. Perhaps the cathedral respected our efforts, because even after all these years the graffiti is still on display.

Long after I was gone, a placard was put on the pew to acknowledge the contributions made by Herbert Cecil and Edith Constance Franklin to education of the cathedral's choristers. However, it was slightly skewed out of position – I assume so that you can still see my name carved into the wood. I take great pride that my name is still there today, and recommend you to look for it the next time you visit the cathedral.

That cathedral choir played a tremendous part in my life, from childhood through to the present day. Being in the choir taught me discipline, which was good for young boys, and we all benefitted from learning how to sing. We had the elderly lay clerks to set an example, and of course I loved the music to the songs we sang.

The discipline learnt at such an early age set me in good stead for the later years of my life and I still try, wherever possible, to assist financially to help in the upkeep of this beautiful cathedral. I hope many future generations can enjoy it also. I firmly believe that it is vital we try to protect our heritage, this being part of that.

You will come to understand through reading my story, how passionate I was, and still am, at helping to restore and maintain buildings of importance. Not just in England, but also in Venice, which is extremely dear to my heart too.

Another lifelong passion that was born while at King's School was field hockey. I started playing aged 13, and my position was half-back. I took to it immediately, and although I regrettably never represented the county, I was something of a natural. I played for King's in many a hotly contested battle with rival schools in Peterborough, Wisbech, Stamford and Oundle, and loved the camaraderie of being part of 11 men on a sporting team.

As well as playing hockey and rugby, I was also a keen cricketer. This was perhaps the weakest of my three sporting loves, but one I still enjoyed tremendously. I fondly remember taking part in the Jaidka Cup – a keenly contested cricket competition in my hometown. What made the tournament more special to me was it was named after the splendid doctor who had delivered me as a baby, Dr K Jaidka.

He was a welcome trend-setter as one of the city's first Asian physicians. Dr Jaidka played a huge role in our close-knit community. As well as being many people's doctor, he was the president of the Peterborough Cricket League, and set up the tournament as a way of increasing league funds in 1934. During my childhood there were lots of inspirational men like Dr Jaidka who served the community; how we could do with more of that spirit in these more insular days.

Back at school, I was a good academic and incredibly social. In time, I was named a prefect, then house captain (of Tudor) before eventually being named the head boy of the school – a great honour! I was surprised to be given it, but had secretly longed for that day for many moons. My parents must have been proud, but the news was not greeted with much obvious excitement.

5
MY RATIONAL
WARTIME DIET

The Second World War provided a strange backdrop for my childhood years. Even my inspirational headmaster Harry Hornsby was sent to serve with the Gurkhas in Burma. We kept in touch through letters, a rare thing for a head to keep up with a student, but something we both enjoyed. I still have those letters to this day. Mr Hornsby was ably replaced by the physics teacher Mr Shearcroft, who handled the school well in his absence.

In Peterborough there was a persistent threat of bombers and fighters overhead, and we would often sleep on top of Morrison shelters or underneath Anderson shelters. But as with so much of my life, food gives me my warmest wartime memories.

Sweets and food were in scarce supply, as was meat – although that obviously didn't affect me one iota. In fact, it was quite a benefit to my parents and sister. My vegetarianism, forever a fated blessing, helped them get more out of our family rations. They got four servings of meat for their three meat-eating mouths. Although I didn't like the idea of them eating animals, I was pleased to help them maximise their rations.

We all had ration books, and that certainly taught me the importance of making the most of what you have and not taking things for granted. But, more than that, I learnt from my father how to get around the most difficult of circumstances in the pursuit of good food.

Thanks to his job taking him all over the Fens, he knew some kindly farmers who he persuaded to help out feeding his often discussed family members. Our rations were a measly two ounces of butter per week, but thanks to my father's agricultural connections he would bring home a whole pound of delicious fresh produce.

On one occasion, a farmer from Whittlesey gave him half a pig to serve to our family. My father stuffed the blessed thing into the boot of his car and covered it with blankets, as it was unlawful to be hoarding such an animal for additional food during the war, then headed home with a heavy foot on the accelerator.

Halfway home, he glanced in his rear view mirror and spotted – as fate would inevitably have it – an approaching police car. If they found him with half a pig he would be in serious trouble. The coppers followed him along that long, straight Fenland road for so long that he was sure something was up. As he toyed with pulling over and admitting his crime before it was discovered, the police car pulled off at a junction and he realised he had gotten away with it.

My relieved father then rushed to the house and told us of his near-miss… all the while covered in a stressful, sweat-drenched shirt. The efforts he went to were amazing, and I think it sowed seeds for my entrepreneurial spirit when it comes to food.

Restaurants had to struggle, but struggle they did. Some results were noteworthy, specifically the success of the communal kitchens known as British Restaurants. We didn't go out to eat in restaurants as a child, something I never questioned.

I was of course aware that the war stretched far beyond my hometown. We used to hear the planes flying over to Coventry and my third cousin Bob Baxter was stationed in the Far East. He usually lived in St Mark's Street, Peterborough, and was gone for so long he didn't see us (or his wife) for four years.

Occasionally, the regrettable backdrop of growing up in the war would rear its head, when you would hear an attack on the streets. I remember bullets being fired by German bombers, but my parents did a good job in shielding me from the full extent of the horrors. I later learnt that many injuries and several deaths were caused by air raids in Peterborough – in 1941 alone one person died on 15 January and another two on 10 May.

As testament to how safe my parents helped me feel, I rarely got out of my bed to go to the shelters when the air-raid sirens blared. With hindsight, this was extremely irresponsible. I vividly remember my sister, mother and father rushing to the shelters when the sirens went off. Yet I ignored their persistent screams to join them, and remained lying in my own bed.

Perhaps refusing to go into the air raid shelters was me avoiding the reality of the situation, even if looking back it was a deathly way to seek such a thing. Goodness knows what worries that caused my parents, but it was a precursor for my bloody mindedness in later life.

We all had gas masks, but we never wore them, thankfully. There was the occasional bomb in Peterborough, and I remember the panic one day when a German bomber was reported targeting Park Road and Broadway, just yards from my family home. There were a lot of cases like that, but I don't remember harm coming to anyone I knew during the conflict.

During the war, King's School was used as a reception centre for evacuees. We would cram into the headmaster's study for updates from Prime Minister Neville Chamberlain on the war effort. A lot changed at school during the war – we lost our school uniforms (except for school caps).

Academic lessons were swapped for digging air-raid trenches around the school playing field and Park Crescent (now part of the Regional College), under the eagle eye of our history teacher 'Shiny' Joe Carruthers.

There were lighter moments, too. One warm memory came during one Christmas towards the tail end of the war. My father had gone to the pub to share a yuletide pint with his friends, and returned in time for Christmas dinner. Only he didn't return on his own, he brought a guest – who happened to be an Italian who was in the country as a prisoner of war.

I forget the chap's name, but they had met in the pub. There were a lot of Italian prisoners of war in Peterborough at that time. Of course, 25 December was an awful day to be a captive in a foreign land, so far from your loved ones. So my father invited him back to our house and he joined us for Christmas dinner. He was the first Italian I ever met, and it was quite fitting that it was around a dining table.

Another new face my father brought home from the pub during the war would go on to become a very dear friend. One evening he returned with an American soldier named Gene who we all became firm friends with, to the point where my father was asked to be best man at his wedding. Gene married a local girl in Wisbech during the war, and my father was proud as punch to be invited to do the honours.

The only problem was, soon after we arrived we learned that Gene already had a wife… this was a bigamist wedding! Apparently this was quite common back in the States, or so he maintained. My parents were incredibly embarrassed by this fact, but to me it was a hilarious and somewhat glamorous revelation.

Gene continued to be a regular visitor throughout the war. He was a valuable resource because his US army rations opened us up to a world we were otherwise denied. He would bring us exotic things like tinned fruits, nylon and chewing gum. Again, another clever little way my father found a way to get around those wartime restrictions.

When the war finished in 1945, there was a tremendous celebration. We had a huge party in the city centre where the whole of Peterborough came together in an almighty mixture of joy, relief and desperate hope that the peace would stay forever. Obviously we were delighted that our troops would be coming home after serving so diligently, and I was personally relieved because, as a 15-year-old, the imminence of my national service had started to linger over me like a shadow that I was glad to escape.

CHAPTER II:
A CONTINENTAL WANDERLUST

The second step in making a pizza is to wait for the bread to bake. Before your ingredients are sprinkled on the top, the body of the pizza must be given time to rise.

This is analogous to the way one should start their professional life. In the same way that a bread must be given time to form a strong foundation of a pizza, a career also takes time to grow. In your formative professional years, you learn from others, and also from your own mistakes.

By rushing a pizza or a career, you will be forever hampered by failing to have a strong base. So take your time – but never stop growing.

6
MY FIRST ITALIAN ADVENTURE

Three years after the war ended, I finished my studies at King's School and embarked on a life-changing trip to stay with the Uzielli di Mari family in Italy. It's strange now to think that our two nations had only recently been fighting in a war, but in 1948 I was offered the chance to spend a summer between school and joining the army to help look after their four children.

I learnt about the opportunity after one of the few female teachers at King's, Mrs Rhume, spoke excitedly to Mr Hornsby about an opportunity available with some of her friends in Italy. Mrs Rhume had somehow got connected with the well-to-do Uzielli di Maris, who were bigwigs in the Italian military. The patriarch Giovanni was a leading admiral in the Italian navy, and he and his wife Maria wanted an English boy to teach the language to their young children.

Mr Hornsby recommended me as a fitting candidate for this extremely rare, glamorous adventure. I immediately accepted the offer, despite not speaking a word of Italian or understanding quite what I was getting myself into.

But I followed my guts that this was a once-in-a-lifetime opportunity, and dived headfirst in to commit to living with them for three months after I finished my exams that summer. As it would turn out, following my often-illogical instincts would eventually prove to be one of my most positive personality traits in adult life.

It wasn't as easy then as it is now to get over to Italy – but it was considerably more fun. I find the way you are treated in airports quite impersonal and hurried. My debut trip to fair Italia was far more exciting – a bus to Dover, a ferry to Calais, a bus to Paris, and then a train all the way to Florence.

It was September 1948, and the family was waiting for me when I rolled into the station. I was greeted first by Giovanni and Maria, who to my great relief both spoke excellent English. It soon became apparent that Giovanni and Maria were real elites and incredibly well educated – quite why they wanted a boy from Peterborough to teach their children was beyond me.

They then introduced me to their delightful children, who I would end up spending so much time with. They were the twin boys Lorenzo and Stefano (both 12), Andrea (10) and little Sophia (7).

The family were based in Florence, where they had a magnificent home with live-in maids and a (very skilled) chef. But they also had an incredibly luxurious second home on the coast. That house was in Forte dei Marmi, a small town not far from Pisa.

Forte dei Marmi had about 5,000 residents, but their population soared during the summer. There can be three times that amount during the hot months, when people flocked to its luxurious Tuscan coast.

We went back and forth between Florence and Forte dei Marmi, and in both places I was smitten with Italian life. I truly valued their warm and friendly nature and immersed myself into their culture and traditions. I bought a bicycle to travel around and mix with the locals, although the conversations were generally in English (with the occasional smattering of French).

The Italians were just excited to meet an English person and wanted to make me feel welcome. In time, I was teaching English to a whole range of youngsters my own age, and even invited them to join the Uzielli di Mari children and I for formal grammar lessons in both of the family homes.

This sparked a lifelong friendship and companionship I have shared with Italians. They are a warm breed of people and I get on with them very well. I agreed with their very patriarchal, male dominated system – although they do also appreciate the many skills and beauty of women (an interest I also retain as an octogenarian).

A number of girls took a fancy to me when I was over there. I suppose it relates to 'peacock theory' – whereby people stand out if they are something different. My English accent certainly helped me to stand out, and I enjoyed numerous flings with Italian lovers that summer. I must confess now to not being able to remember any of their names, but in hindsight that is hopefully forgivable due to their large quantity and short respective tenures.

Again though, the main purpose for me being in Italy was to interact socially with the family's four children. Most days were spent having fun and playing with them. I was very warmly taken in and treated like a long lost fifth sibling. They were fascinated to be able to talk with an English boy and they picked up the language very quickly.

I must say I picked up some Italian, but at a slower rate than the children learnt my mother tongue. It seemed their young brains were like sponges, whereas my teenage one was already seemingly a little bit clogged up.

It was within the family home that I was finally exposed to the thing that would well and truly change my life: fresh, home-made pizza. Even in Italy, pizza was not as readily available in the 1940s as it is in Scotland in the 2010s. It was a treat, and although I had heard of the dish it was not served to me until my going-away party in December 1948.

How I would come to wish I had been privy to it earlier.

The family were big meat eaters, and their chef would serve me up pasta and vegetables while they had their family meals. Even that was more exciting than the cumbersome, clunky meals I ate back in England at the expense of my mother's fine meat dishes.

But the true eye-opener was to come during my leaving party, when the family chef prepared a pizza for me and the children. I had seen these dishes before – my new-found Italian friends and I would go to watch a highly skilled young man named Benito tossing pizzas high into the air in one of the restaurants. He wore a distinctive black and white horizontally striped shirt, which I remember thinking looked impressively smart for a cook.

My friends explained to me that Benito was a 'pizzaiolo' – a chef who makes pizzas. I couldn't think of any other food whose chefs had a specialist name.

But I never ate one of Benito's pizzas. It would be an affront to the family, who always insisted on cooking for me. But I was most intrigued by his fantastic preparation methods, slapping the dough around, tossing the base around the kitchen and liberally splashing the ingredients on top. It was almost like a dance.

I had told the family how much I enjoyed watching Benito, and as a surprise for my leaving bash they organised to have a pizza made in their home.

It was an authentic mozzarella, with the bread kneaded by hand. It was in the classic circular shape but far larger than one you may have seen. It was the most appetising thing I had ever had before. In the six decades since I must have enjoyed thousands of pizzas, but I still remember that first one.

As well as kick-starting a life-long love for pizzas, the trip gave me a life-long connection to Italy. I would later take many 'business trips' to the country that bordered on personal holidays, and still try to get back as often as possible. I have also stayed in touch with the family who made it all possible – especially Lorenzo.

When he became an adult, the 12-year-old boy I helped to tutor decided to move just up the road from me in England to run a hotel in Louth. From Florence to Lincolnshire… what a change in scenery!

7
FROM THE SAHARA TO THE STUDENTS' UNION

Luckily, my own change in scenery was rather different after leaving Italy. I already had my place waiting for me at the University of Cambridge but before that I had to do my national service in the British Army, stationed in Egypt.

First I had to pass my training in England, which took eight months and was quite a quick process, before I was sent out by boat to Africa at 19 years of age.

I was to be stationed there for a further nine months, and took to army life well. I was in the Royal Artillery and Royal Army Service Corps, where I progressed to the rank of Second lieutenant. My platoon included 20 people and we were stationed in the desert. Our job was keeping the peace. To be honest, this was not an arduous task, as we saw very little of Egyptian people.

I was living in luxury in Italy, but came back to Earth thanks to the fairly squalid surroundings in Egypt – as was to be expected. We slept in tents pitched in the Sahara and got by on basic army food rations.

My budding romance with pizza had to be suspended – sadly there were none to be seen in Egypt. But I suffered less than most because I was used to limited dinners through my self-imposed vegetarianism.

Aside from larking about in the barracks, I had never driven before. That was to change very dramatically during my service. One day I was called into my commanding officer's tent. He handed me an envelope and said it was a very important note that had to be taken to Alexandria urgently. The only problem was that I was in the middle of the desert, and Alexandria was hundreds of miles away in the north.

My commanding officer told me to take one of their motorbikes right away. Ignoring the consequence of my own honesty, I decided it was best to tell the commanding officer that I could not drive. He replied by bellowing, "What do you mean you can't drive?" to which I said I have never had a driving licence or a driving lesson. He said, "Well that doesn't mean you can't drive, does it?" and promptly sent me on my way.

So I jumped onto the motorbike and set off!

At first I thought my debut ride was to be one of the shortest in history – I almost fell off the blessed thing three times in a minute. But I soon just about got the hang of it and, some eight or nine hours later arrived in one piece to deliver the note. I still have no idea what the note said, but it's strange that now it could be sent with the click of a button on the internet. However, that seems immeasurably less exciting than a motoring novice delivering it after racing across the desert on a motorbike.

While we were there I did get to go to Cairo on a break, where I sailed on the River Nile and saw the pyramids and the great tombs. But it was very much a service of duty in Egypt, and I was relieved when my tenure came to an end after nine months. I sailed back to Britain, where I was due to start studying at the University of Cambridge.

I enrolled thanks to a choral-cum-history exhibition – a fancy name for a scholarship. My time there was one of the great features of my life. How great it was when I was accepted.

It was much harder to get into a university in those days, and that was a proud day for my parents also. It was seen as something very special to send your son or daughter to university, and Cambridge was the top one, in my opinion. My father expressed his thoughts, as he often would, through a touching letter that he pressed into my hand on the day I started university. It told me how life is good and to enjoy it. I vowed to do so.

I actually had been granted the choice of two Cambridge colleges and two at Oxford. An innate magnetism pulled me towards St Catharine's, Cambridge, and after I made my decision was later pleased to hear that fellow Peterborian Dr John Addenbrooke had studied there. He amassed a wealth of knowledge that would go on to see him inspire the eponymous hospital in Cambridge.

'Cats', as we called it, was a reasonably humble college with some more famous brothers on Kings Parade. It was next to King's College, opposite Corpus and adjacent to the Queen's College at the rear – truly magnificent surroundings. But despite these illustrious neighbours, I was a Cats man, and took great pride in singing every Sunday in the college chapel.

I can't say that I worked as hard as I could have done, or got the grades that I could have achieved. But it was a great experience that I would not change for the world. Cats was a great place to have a social life, and my good friend Ron Simson and I would gallivant around the pubs with girls until all hours of the morning.

Ron was a thinly built Scotsman who studied engineering and would eventually help me to establish

PizzaExpress. Indeed, it was Ron who would eventually advise me to ditch square pizzas on greaseproof in favour of circular ones on flats. But back then, he was a good drinking buddy who was a great partner in crime for meeting girls.

He had missed out on National Service after being passed unfit, but he was certainly fit as a drinking buddy. We basically drank a lot and then went carousing. There were no mixed colleges so we would have to climb over other colleges' walls to see girls, and then sneak out before being caught. I have never been short of lady friends.

Girls were almost like a sport in those days, but not my only athletic pursuit. I represented Cats in rugby, field hockey and rowing (albeit on the fifth boat crew). It was a great time, but I missed watching my beloved Peterborough United playing football. It always gave me a good excuse to head back to Peterborough once a term on the number 151 bus to catch a game.

My choral-cum-history exhibition meant that I sang in the choir on Sunday evenings – a most pleasant experience. Also in the choir was Peter Le Huray – a far more talented musician there on an organ scholarship who would find later fame as a musicologist and author.

My artistic exploits were perhaps less traditional, and I was well known to sing raucous songs about our beloved Cats College. 'The Cats Whiskers' were a multitude of songs that wouldn't seem out of place on a first team rugby tour, with outrageous lyrics dripping with the sort of innuendo that would make a sailor blush.

One of the naughtier versions went like this;

"We are cats on the roof tops, cats on the tiles,
"Cats with syphilis, cats with piles
"Cats with their arseholes wreathed in smiles,
"As we revel in the joys of copulation!"

In the first year we had to live in digs. I stayed in a one-bedroom flat on 67 Beech Road, just outside of the centre of town, and would cycle to the college every day. My landlords were a fine local couple called Mr and Mrs Fitch, and I was very content with the basic room and board they offered.

My application to get a dorm inside the college was accepted the next year, and I ended up getting a very splendid room overlooking the King's Parade. It was a magnificent room that was situated at the main arch of the college, and made it impossible to not get involved in its social life.

My links to the college were retained through the years and I was always keen to donate cash to Cats after I made my money. I am honoured to say that many decades later, there is now a life-size portrait of myself in a prominent location inside St Catherine's. I was also made a Fellow which allowed me to walk on the grass – quite an honour.

8
THE BIRTH OF A SALESMAN

Once my three years were completed at Cambridge, it became time to get a job in the real world in the summer of 1953. I didn't remotely know what I wanted to do yet, but you have to get a job when you graduate so I started looking around.

As much as I enjoyed my studies I didn't really want to be a historian. Too much living in the past, I wanted to make things happen in the present (and future).

Soon after finishing my studies I landed a job with a company called Tiger Toys. They were based in the West Country and, as you could expect from their catchy name, sold wooden animal toys for young children. My starting job was a salesman for this company, which had nothing at all to do with my history degree... perfect!

But a job is a job, and I felt confident in my abilities. I have always had a gift of the gab, as they say, and I took to the position and quickly established myself as one of their top salesman.

In the days before computers and cars that talk to you to give you directions, the job was a bit of a logistical headache. I would first have to get my hands on a phone book from the place I was going to, and pinpoint all of the toy shops there.

I would write the address down in a little book (along with the phone number, in case I couldn't find it), and then pull out a map to draw my route. This was all good fun and I enjoyed the sense of adventure, plotting my sales all over the United Kingdom.

I would drive all over the country in my clapped out old car, and map out where all the toy shops were in each city, town or village along the way. These were back in the days when you would have a lot more independent retailers and less mammoth, impersonal shops like Toys 'R' Us.

The people behind the counter were businessmen, not spotty teenagers only there to get a bit of beer money. The decision about what to sell was made by them, not a think-tank in an ivory tower in some distant foreign land.

That meant they were my target. I needed to make that trader see the value of that wooden horse I was trying to sell him – to show him why my wooden horse would appeal to Mrs Barbara Braddock from Broad Street, and why her young son Billy would love to receive it as a present.

I approached every shop with enthusiasm, confidence and self-belief that I was going to make a sale. I think the most important thing for a salesman is to be sure of themselves, and create a belief that the product is worthy of the other person's interest.

Enthusiasm is contagious, and there were few shopkeepers who could get shot of me without buying anything from a single item to a whole case worth of goods.

Another tip for any aspiring salesman reading this book is to learn about your product inside and out. You have to know what you are selling and be able to counter any and every possible reason somebody may have to say no. That may sound obvious, but you would be surprised by how many people do not master the basics of a profession before they try to break new ground within it.

I think I was quite lucky to be a salesman in the 1950s. I was able to think about the product, imagine negative responses and consider fast rebuttals to uninterested shopkeepers. Nowadays, I dare say salesmen are all cold-calling relentlessly on the telephone and don't have a moment to stop and think about their pitch. Sales must be a colder, less engaging profession now due to the improvements in technology. No wonder advertising is so important – that is where the real sales are made now.

But back in the 1950s, it gave me great excitement at the start of each journey to load up the boot of my car knowing that on the way back home it would be much lighter again.

It was my own personal challenge to sell all those toys, and more often than not, I did. But I knew all along that the job was not my calling. Elements of being a salesman appealed to me, but I still had a yearning for the continent and felt that was where I would find my destiny.

How to get there was proving the tricky thing… until a quite remarkable opportunity fell into my lap.

9
LIFE ON THE SEA

My work took me down to the London docks one afternoon and I got talking to some of the dockers. We were chatting about what life was like on the sea, where they had got to, and how I was interested in doing something similar.

The good fortune came when I revealed that I was from Peterborough and they replied by saying their skipper was as well. They said because we came from the same small city he would love to talk to me. It was a quite remarkable co-incidence. As so often seems the case, an opportunity fell into my lap. But I believe the important thing is not the luck of getting an opportunity – it's having the guts to grasp it.

Although the skipper (Captain Nigel Parkinson) was from Peterborough and was in charge of this boat (The Yarvic), he was not in London at that time. Captain Parkinson was due to return to London the next day before setting off to France, yet I was 100 miles from home and not expected back in the capital for weeks. Undeterred, and committed to making the most of this wonderful co-incidence, I decided not to drive west that night to my home, but instead sleep rough on the docks.

That night under the stars proved to be a great investment. The next morning I met with Captain Parkinson (and his charming wife Pamela), who ignored my dishevelled state from a night on the streets and instantly took a shine to me.

We chatted about our shared Peterborough heritage, and he offered me the job of deck hand on the Yarvic. The ship would be sailing to and from London to Paris (via the Seine), and the position was mine to start immediately. I jumped at the chance.

Without so much as returning back home, I took the job and my spot on the good ship Yarvic. There was a crew of around 10 good men, and our job was carrying things from the British Embassy to Paris, and then collecting Pan Books for the return voyage.

The ships sailed to Paris every fortnight – meaning there were over 20 return trips over the choppy English Channel every year. The skipper ran an informal crew and urged us to call him 'Nigel'. It was great fun, going past Le Havre and through the seven locks on the way to gay Paris. We would tie up at a lock en route and sneak into a local bistro for a spot of supper. Slim, the first mate, would take care of the ship until our return. It was as idyllic as it sounds!

What fun it was, and Nigel and Pamela were such inspirations to us all. The passage wasn't always easy though. Although sturdy, The Yarvic was a small boat and there were many occasions in high winds when I thought it was going to capsize. I was a decent swimmer but didn't fancy that idea of swimming the 21 miles of the English Channel very much.

I was part of a small group of nomadic exiles which in the mid-1950s had no collective name. We were ahead of the somewhat clichéd 1960s era of beatniks and hippies. We didn't dress with a uniform 'uniqueness' – our hair was not in beads, we wore smart clothes not jeans, and most of us felt it was our duty to find a job.

Whenever we would arrive in Paris, we would look for a hotel to crash in. Rates were cheap and we would bunk into shared rooms (unless we found a pretty Parisian girl whose room we could share). One of the big bonuses of these trips to the French capital was it gave me a chance to explore and expand upon my love of jazz music – New Orleans style.

I was keen on jazz for as long as I can remember, but you would only really hear proper players on records while in Peterborough or Cambridge. Here, in Paris, you would have the greatest jazz musicians in the world appearing at cafés and bars all over the city (especially in the St. Germain quarter). I couldn't get enough of it, and gorged on live performances on a nightly basis.

While I had gained academic benefits through singing, I had never mastered playing an instrument. It was in Paris that I decided I should put an end to that. The French made top class instruments and I found my way to a lovely little shop called 'La Maison de Musique'. I told the shop's almost stereotypically glamorous owner that I was taken by a clarinet I had seen.

I was desperate to get one but was disappointed when she quoted the high price it would cost. I forget now how much it was, but I recall telling her I would only be able to afford half of it on my modest income. The job was more about experiences than money, and I wasn't compensated terribly well for my time.

The lady took pity on me and said, "Well you can pay half now and come back to pay off the rest when you have the money". I was astounded at her gesture of good will and faith that I would return. When I asked again if she was sure, she told me that she trusted me because I was an English gentleman.

It's remarkable how this country's estimation on foreign soil has dropped since then. I blame it on cheap, booze-filled holidays where the desire is no longer to mix with the culture; it is to impose drunken loutish behaviour onto the locals. But these were different times, and I gladly accepted her kind offer. Of course, I promised to return to the shop to pay the second half of the debt when I came back to Paris two weeks (and one pay cheque) later.

That was over 50 years ago, but I have always kept that clarinet and it sits to this day in the living room of my flat in Peterborough. It still carries a fine tune over five decades later, and I often think of the kind help that shopkeeper gave me to afford the clarinet while playing it. Indeed, such generosity would later inspire much of my own philanthropy later in life.

My dream of running a pizza restaurant was really born when I was in Paris. It was the first place I had ever lived where pizzas were not only readily available, but I had enough independence and cash to indulge in them.

In Italy they were seen as a cheap dish that took up a disproportionate amount of a busy chef's time. And it was therefore that I learnt with great delight that pizzerias were commonplace and inexpensive in the Germain quarter of Paris. Somewhat impecunious, I was delighted to chance upon at least a dozen inexpensive pizzerias and, inevitably, became addicted to a splendid, bustling place in Rue St Benoit, a street at the beating heart of Saint-Germain-des-Prés.

There were clearly an increasing number of pizzerias springing up around the French capital, presumably because the standard of their haute cuisine was becoming more difficult to maintain. At the same time, pizza was extremely simple and profitable for the restaurant owners.

More importantly, it was a treasure trove for a vegetarian, and pizzas rapidly became my main gastronomic delight. Our group of 10 shipmates were all living out of suitcases in hotels and hostels, and as such we would go out looking for a restaurant most nights. Sure enough, most nights I would use my salesman nous to persuade the others into testing out the many pizzerias.

With the job the way it was we were always on the move. A couple of nights in Paris then back on the boat, a day or two getting back to London and then pitching up in the docks. It was a fast-paced, all-action job and one that was a really excellent experience.

But sadly, it was not without its dark moments.

Nigel had grown terribly sick, despite only being a man in his 40s. About three months after I took the job he stopped travelling with us. Pamela also stopped coming on the trips, so she could tend to Nigel as he lay ill. They had a fancy flat in Earls Court, London, where I spent a few nights at their invitation. Tragically, he lost his battle with illness and died soon after. Pamela became a widow far too early in life.

In all the turmoil the ship needed a new captain, and I was shocked when Pamela asked me to take the reins. At this stage I had been on boats for less than six months and was still in my mid-20s. But Pamela said Nigel had seen something in me that made him think I could lead men, and I was put in charge of the boat. This was a great honour.

But as much as I enjoyed the job, this lofty promotion served to make me question again whether it was really what I wanted to do with my life.

Such questions must have driven my mother mad – I had walked away from a prosperous job to pursue my pipe dreams of travelling. Then when the travelling job started to look prosperous, I again started looking elsewhere. But my mother was nothing if not supportive, and she never once tried to rein in my desires.

And so, it was no surprise really when I handed in my notice to Pamela a few months after being made captain of The Yarvic. I was sad to go, but felt a life on the seas was not why God had put me on Earth. I look back on my time on the boat with great warmth, and am proud to have been listed as a sailor on Lloyd's List – a legacy that far outlasted my tenure in the industry.

10
A WORKING BEATNIK DRIFTING THROUGH EUROPE

By the late 1950s I was in my mid–20s and decided it was time to give Italy a proper try as an adult. It had been a dream to commit to the Italian way of life since those all-too-brief months between school and the army, and now I was old enough to give it a go.

While the destination was great, I was heading over there virtually penniless… and with no work lined up. The job on the boat was more fun than it was profitable, so I had no savings – and no choice but to hitch-hike my way across Europe to get to the promised land of Rome. I'd just stick my thumb up on the eastward-facing side of the motorway and see who was heading towards Italy.

I managed to get from Paris to Rome in just two days, thanks to a few lifts from some kindly strangers going in the right direction. When I arrived I was similarly lacking in preparation. I paid to put an advert into the Roman newspaper, and rubbed together just enough coins to find lodgings for my first night. It was less than salubrious.

There I was, cramped in a tiny shoebox room on the wrong side of the tracks in Rome with five Italian bricklayers. Yet I couldn't be happier, because I was finally in Rome. The labourers rose noisily at the crack of dawn, and I soon followed. Luckily, my advert proved successful and a splendid old local man named Cavaliere Sciappone contacted me at the hostel.

He asked if I could sell some items off his barrow. He would push it all over Rome, and had a mixed stock of post cards, earth allegedly from the Catacombs and trinkets, all weighed down with a lumpy horseshoe. They were interesting, if dubious, souvenirs.

Signor Sciappone told me that he kept the vehicle in the same place that Emperor Nero had kept his chariot. Inspired by this brush with the Empire, I cheekily wrote a note saying 'SHOE FROM JULIUS CAESAR'S HORSE, 5000 LIRE', and attached it to the horseshoe that served as a paperweight.

The tongue-in-cheek advert was written in English, and had been meant as a joke for any tourists. But, within an hour, something quite unexpected occurred. An American couple came by, and the husband's eyes exploded when he saw the note. "Honey, look, a shoe that belonged to Julius Caesar's horse!"

They obviously believed it and, with a big smile on their faces, said they must have it. So I said, well you can read the sign, that will be 5,000 lire – the equivalent of £15 today. They handed over the money and took the paperweight, no doubt delighted at the thought of how much this trinket from Europe would impress their friends back in America.

I like to think that the horseshoe is now a family heirloom that sits pride of place in a living room somewhere in Kentucky.

When I told Sr Sciappone of the sale, he joyously said that it was "money from heaven". The next day, the wily old entrepreneur brought along a dozen horseshoes threaded on a piece of wire. He told me that we were now selling a whole range of shoes that belonged to Caesar's horses. They flew off the shelves – rather than being the paperweight for his trinkets, they were now his most demanded item!

It was a slightly dubious practice, but taught me an important business lesson. You should always cater supply to meet demand, or "smell what sells", as we would later say in London.

The story of Caear's horseshoes spread around like wildfire, and we ended up getting a visit from two American journalists from the Associated Press – one was a reporter, the other a photographer. I told them that I was a Cambridge University graduate, and the thought of an Oxbridge alumnus selling from a barrow in central Rome must have caught their imagination.

They ran a humorous article on me, and the story was so popular that it ended up appearing in the *Daily Mail* and then my hometown paper, the *Peterborough Evening Telegraph*. How the boys back home must have laughed!

After the story went global, I met up for a drink with the reporter and his photographer. They told me they were looking for a clerk to work in their newsroom. This seemed a steady job, and journalists are always interesting people to be around, so I thought, 'What the hell' and said I'd like to apply.

Before even sending in my CV, I was summoned to the editor's office the next day, and he offered me the job on the spot.

The role was proofreading copy, organising meetings for the editors and answering phones (which never stopped ringing with people who thought they had the next day's front page scoop). The office was full of Americans, who lived by the fine philosophy of 'work hard, party hard'.

The days were long, but boy were they fun!

I had never experienced madness like that of working in a newsroom. Although I stayed in the office, the reporters and photographers jetted off on jobs incessantly through the day. That one little office had to document every major incident happening in the city, so you can realise just how stretched we were. We would all rush around for hours, often without sitting down let alone a chance to grab any food.

Once you arrived in the morning there would be a news list of the expected jobs – a restaurant opening here, a football match there. But what you don't account for is that the news cannot be scripted, and that list was never what actually happened. Tomorrow's paper can't be predicted yesterday.

Although there would be a news conference at 8am to give the news editor an idea of how the day should pan out, jobs would come in on top of the initial workload throughout the day. So, as well as covering the opening of a new pizzeria in Nomentano and the Lazio football game, we would be getting calls in from people about a five-car pile-up on the Viale Giulio Cesare, or the nut threatening tourists at the Coliseum with a knife.

Rome needed more than seven days per week to report on its seven hills.

Ever the workaholic, I kept my job with Sr Sciappone as well, so I would go from my 8am to 6pm role in the office to an evening of shifting trinkets in the market square. Within a month, I had gone from being a sailor to selling Julius Caesar's horseshoes to Americans while working for the Associated Press. It was a good time to be young and money could be earned while having fun. I worry that today's graduates get somewhat onto the career conveyor belt before they have even lived a little, which is a great shame.

When I look back on that period the thing that sticks in my head most, quite fittingly I suppose, is how hungry I always was. Here I was, living in the very country that made me realise that there is good food out there for a vegetarian… and I was working eight hour shifts on one job, going straight to a five hour shift on the stall… and eating very little. But, at that time, I suppose my work ethic was greater than my hunger.

Whenever the busy working day was over, I would sneak off to the nearest pizzeria or trattoria, where I could polish off a full pizza with a litre-and-a-half of wine. The thought of my upcoming supper kept me going through those long, relentless days.

But that thought was not quite enough for me in the longer term, and again I soon found myself looking in the newspaper classifieds for other jobs. I saw an advert in one of the international newspapers for a job with an organisation named the American Book Distributors. The company were from Chicago, but they were looking for a sales representative to manage its European operations.

Preferably I would have stayed in Rome, but the job was based in Frankfurt, Germany. It was basically heading up a team that would try to sell American servicemen books that reminded them of their home life, and would take the successful applicant to every European country that had an American base.

I duly applied and they were good enough to send a representative to Rome for the interview. Like most Yanks, he was most impressed by the fact I was a

Cambridge graduate. We talked mainly about that, although I tried to shoehorn in as much of my experiences travelling across Europe and being a salesman; it seemed the two graduate letters after my name were more appealing to him than my real-life anecdotes.

That proved to be my last ever official job interview.

I suspect that they are a little bit different nowadays. Having a degree back then was like saying you were a superhero, but now they seem two-a-penny and do not hold the same reverence as they once did. But my Cambridge degree impressed them very much, and I was offered the job.

The salary was considerably more than my combined wages in Italy and, although I was sad to leave the Old Boot behind just a few months after arriving, it was a great opportunity. Also, as was the case with much of my youthful wanderlust, I saw Germany as another blank canvas – another country offering another adventure.

They say that a rolling stone gathers no moss. Well, after migrating to my fourth country in less than a decade, my pebble would have been as smooth as a new-born baby's bottom.

11
AN ENTREPRENEURIAL SPARK

lthough I would have to leave vibrant Rome, the job jumped out to me because I was confident of my abilities. I had already worked as a salesman for Tiger Toys and for Sr Sciappone, and I had already shown that I could handle the travelling lifestyle.

The American Book Distributors flogged encyclopaedias and other books of knowledge on the US Army bases. Their biggest title was Compton's Pictured Encyclopaedia, a comprehensive corpus of trivia that had become an American institution since it was first published in 1922.

There were new volumes printed every couple of years – such was the increasing quest for knowledge, an impossible-to-reach itch that will never be scratched. As a result, it was with great excitement that the American troops would react when I rolled into their base with the latest version for them.

I suppose it was a way for them to feel normal when they were based halfway across the world serving their country in some foreign field.

It was the perfect job for me – extra chance to travel all over the continent while still plying my trade as a salesman. The bases were all over Europe, and I would be on perpetual loops that saw me jump from Switzerland to Germany to Lichtenstein. Remember that while this was before the EU expansion, it was also before the days of mass bureaucracy, so it was no bother hopping over the borders.

Although I had been taken on as an agent who actively went to the base, I also had some responsibility in the company and they had put me in charge of 40 salesmen. Similar to my job at Tiger Toys, I would provide the workers with the necessary directions around Europe and tools to shift the books to the troops.

I also travelled all around, but my main base was in Frankfurt, Germany. I moved into a very nice flat – number 21 on Rhinestraße, in the Westendstraße area. That was the main hub of the Compton's European operations, but every week we would be going to different countries' army bases to see what we could sell. These loops would see three of four of us cram into a car and drive all around the capitalist countries in Europe – France, Holland, Denmark, Lichtenstein, Belgium... you name it, we went there.

As a consequence, we had many company cars. And boy, did they not hold back on the expense! I mainly drove Jaguars, but also Rolls-Royces, a large Opel and many Citroens. There would be a team of us going to a country, and we would travel with three or four of us in a car on each loop.

At the same time, I was earning quite the pretty penny. While in Germany I bought a Citroen and a Rolls-Royce for my own personal use. Why work for a good wage if you're not going to spend it on good things?

While we were on our trans-national driving loops, I would always insist on being the driver. I loved spinning my wheels through European roads, and could probably have been a trucker if I didn't get the good hand dealt to me by my upbringing. Once we got to the destination, we would stay in the best room in the best hotel they had to offer. It was all on Uncle Sam's dollar, so why not?

On the bases, selling the books was like shooting fish in a barrel. The American soldiers longed for home. I know I was a voluntarily wandering soul, but I could empathise with their homesickness. The difference was, an Englishman in mainland Europe could easily get home. Although today's cheap airlines weren't there to jet you around Europe on a whim, it was easy enough to get back.

These boys didn't have that luxury. They were thousands of miles from their loved ones and had little to no contact with their homeland. That meant when I came knocking on their base with the latest edition of the Compton's Pictured Encyclopaedia, they were desperate to buy it from me.

These were big books that sold for a decent dollar. But it gave them a much-needed feeling of attachment to their own culture. The Encyclopaedia was a summary of what was happening in their world, something they were desperate to get their hands on while over here cleaning up war-weary Europe.

The sales patches were not confined just to the actual bases, and the soldiers would also disperse into lovely little villages. Unlike when I was with Tiger Toys, this was a large scale, professional operation. Whenever I would arrive, the soldiers and officers would have been pre-warned of my intending visit by head office, and they would be fervently expecting my arrival.

The Compton's Picture Encyclopaedia was a huge corpus of a book. It sold at $180 (or you could pay the more affordable 18 payments of $10). I very much enjoyed the enthusiasm the soldiers had when I would arrive – not just because the easy sales meant a healthy commission for myself.

I made many friends while working for Compton's, but one in particular stands out head-and-shoulders above the others. She was Phyllis Senter – a beautiful American woman who was not only the longest romantic partner I had, but also the only person to ever persuade me to eat meat.

I met Phyllis soon after coming to Germany, and was immediately struck by her beauty. She was living with a man named Don Senter, but soon after I arrived our relationship became a romantic one.

We would hit the town, and visit all the German nightclubs, art galleries and restaurants. But our biggest shared passion was jazz music, and it was with Phyllis that I watched the man I believe to be the greatest ever musician – Duke Ellington. He was an unparalleled showman and composer, and despite being in his later years, he was still a mesmeric performer.

It was a good thing that Phyllis also enjoyed jazz and the Duke, because she was a very strong-willed woman and a more enthusiastic debater than a politician talking to a swing voter on the eve of a general election. If Phyllis was alive at the time of the Reformation, she could have taken court at the Diet of Worms and defeated Martin Luther before lunch. After eating, she could have swapped sides and verbally mauled Johann Eck, bringing down both arguments of the Papal schism!

When you went out with Phyllis to an art gallery, you were told quite firmly what was good and what was not. When you went to a concert, she would pass onto you what was commendable in the performance, and what was ghastly. She was not one to sit on the fence, and was so committed to her stance that debates with Phyllis rapidly became incessantly one-sided. Her passions and opinions were also incredibly contagious.

Now it was this ruthless debating skill that led me down the path of doing something I thought I would never do – eating meat.

While visiting the restaurants in Frankfurt, Phyllis would mercilessly rib me for my vegetarianism. As a red-blooded American, she thought it bizarre that a man would choose pasta over pork, and she relentlessly pushed for me to join her in ordering a carnivore's dish.

Eventually, I gave in and ordered a steak. I'm not sure whether it was because I was desperate to impress this wildly effusive woman, or whether I just wasn't in the mood for yet another argument masked as a debate. But for the first time since that trip to see those mild-mannered 'Scottish monsters', I ate some meat.

Of course, I felt bad for eating the steak, but you do strange things when you're in love. I didn't remotely enjoy the meal but chewed it down and feigned a smile; again, there was no sense in debating a contrary stance to Phyllis' opinion.

The fact that I was persuaded to eat steak is a source of great amusement to my sister Wendy. She thinks it a hoot that my loving mother couldn't persuade me to renege on my vegetarian vows with her outstanding cooking, yet one pretty American girl could make me tuck into some steak with no more than the blink ing of her eyelids.

As well as jazz, restaurants and art galleries, we would both go to church together. There was an English-speaking Church of England community there, and its parish was somewhat contradictorily filled with Yanks. Although I picked up a lot of German while I was over, it is startling with hindsight how I was living in Germany but dating, working and worshiping with Americans.

While there I did make good friends with another local called Fred Heeb, who I am still in touch with to this day. He was mutual friends with Bob Jackson – the very wealthy man who headed up the Compton's operation from back in America. Mr Jackson was an influential person to share a mutual friend, but his level was so high I never expected to meet him in person.

The company also flew me over to America for the first time in my life – a fantastic occasion. I was sent over to Chicago about two years into my time with the company to meet with some of the real high-flyers in the company.

When I touched down, the thing that struck me most about Chicago was the remarkable scale of everything. The buildings were all so much bigger and shinier than I had experienced in England, France, Italy and Germany… not surprising, when you think the war had just ravaged those countries.

In one of these mammoth buildings was the Compton's office, where I went to for a meeting. I introduced myself to the receptionist, and she told me the office was some two-thirds of the way up this skyscraper. I hopped into a lift and zipped up dozens of floors to get to the office… a far different prospect to my operations in Frankfurt where the roving Rolls-Royce was my office.

This was my first experience with the people who truly make the wheels of capitalism spin. I had been working for them for months, but it is very different to be taking directions from people rather than seeing how their brains work while looking into their eyeballs.

To my surprise, waiting for me in the luxurious board room was with Fred's pal, Bob Jackson. This was *the* top dog in the company, and it was a great privilege to meet with him – and I dare say a good indication of my standing within Compton's.

I went into that meeting a good salesman, but I came out of it wanting to be an entrepreneur. Mr Jackson imposed onto me a desire to get into this cut-throat capitalist world. He spoke excitedly about expansion plans, desires to make things bigger and better. At this point, my role in the company was essentially a freelance business salesman, but they wanted me to become more like a franchisee.

For all their wants to be an international company, they were very American-focused and didn't really know the best way to go about expanding into European markets, rather than selling to Yanks based there. Mr Jackson didn't so much ask me for my tips, but told me to get thinking about new business models for mainland Europe. I was very excited by his ambition.

The other thing I took from the meeting was how important it was for the leader of a company to work with (not above) their employees. Mr Jackson treated others as his equal and respected them enough to court their ideas. More priceless guidance for my own future use.

I left Mr Jackson's office and headed back to my hotel racking my brain with publishing ideas to bring to Europe. The next day, I went to the airport with my entrepreneurial spark well and truly lit. But then on the long flight back to Frankfurt, I started to digress from thinking of a corporate strategy for Compton's, and started to think it may be time for me to go into business for myself.

Mr Jackson had seen my entrepreneurial spirit and asked me to cultivate it for Compton's, but in reality his pep talk made me realise it was time to stop sitting in the safe zone of working for others and give my own business a go.

The problem was – what would that company be? I didn't know what I wanted to run, but I had a real itch to get something going. It felt like my calling.

After I got back to Frankfurt, I kept my thoughts to myself. I thought it better than telling Phyllis or my colleagues for fear of rocking the boat until I knew exactly what my next step would be. However, again fate intervened, and in a most unexpected and tragic manner: my father died.

We all loved him dearly and his early death in 1964 (at the age of just 57) was a terrible blow. He had lung cancer, brought on from a lifetime of smoking a pipe.

The marvellous Macmillan nurses were a huge support to the family – I don't know what we would have done without them. In his last days they made my father feel as comfortable as possible.

His early death hit us all hard, and my mother never re-married. She needed her family around her – and as a result, I decided that it was time to stop gallivanting around the continent and move back to my homeland. If I was in England, I would certainly be closer to my mother to help comfort her after my father's death. I may also have a greater chance of making my entrepreneurial ambitions come to fruition.

Sadly, a casualty of this decision was Phyllis, who remained in Germany after I told her not to follow me to England. The decision terminated my longest romantic relationship, and was one of many times I put a sense of duty over my own personal pleasure.

And so, in the spring of 1965, I split up with Phyllis and moved back to England.

CHAPTER III:
BRINGING PIZZA TO ENGLAND

After the bread and toppings of your formative pizza are ready, you have completed the preparation. Now it's time to put it to the test – insert it into a piping hot oven and wait for the pizza to cook. If the pizza has been prepared well, it will taste fantastic.

Similarly in one's life, once you have set your principles and learnt through experience, the time for planning is over. Now you need to invest in your dream and see if it comes to reality – this can only happen by diving into your project with both feet. Then you wait to see if it is successful or not...

12
THERE'S NOT A DECENT PIZZERIA IN LONDON

I decided it best to station myself in London – the country's most thriving city, and only 90 minutes by car from my grieving mother in Peterborough. I signed for a room in a house share at number 3 St John's Street, Farringdon, before even finding a job. Although I came to London without employment, I had saved up a fair few pennies from my time on the continent. I arrived determined to enjoy everything the capital had to offer in those swashbuckling days of the swinging '60s.

As ever, I would regularly eat out, and was again lucky enough to fall into the company of some fantastically interesting and inspiring people. My best pal was Noel Terence Graham-Toler, better known as the Earl of Norbury – but known to me simply as 'Poly'.

We met soon after I arrived in London at a swanky party put on by his fiancée Anne Mathew, who had hired out a bar in Clerkenwell with a jazz band playing. Perfect. Anne and Poly were both music connoisseurs and well-travelled, and it was great to reminisce of the thriving jazz scenes abroad. The three of us soon became great friends.

More often than not, we would be drawn to Soho. The borough was bristling with buoyancy – an unofficial gathering point for all the world's populations. There were Germans and Hungarians, Muslims and Bulgarians – all in one street. This was quite alluring to me, because despite being back in England I was rather proud of my nomadic lifestyle and loved to talk to people of all cultures.

Soho was a place that served as an idealistic, idyllic blueprint for multiculturalism. Everyone integrated with one another; all that mattered was who you were – not *what* you were. That is what multiculturalism should be. I worry that today, the phrase has come to mean simply that different cultures exist in the same area, and they 'tolerate' one another. I don't like that word or what it implies.

To 'tolerate' focuses more on a dilution of all cultures rather than a celebration of any. One 'tolerates' slow drivers. One 'tolerates' crying babies. One even 'tolerates' inflation. The word suggests pacifism against something that annoys you. You therefore shouldn't 'tolerate' people from other cultures. You should integrate with them (as they should with you).

And there was nothing that symbolised that wonderful integration better than the restaurants in 1960s Soho. Every heritage was wildly celebrated. You could feed on noodles or whale, chop suey or snail. You could order curry, ham, biscuits or jam. Or winkels and cheese, whatever you please.

Yet, as ever, there was still not a decent pizzeria in sight! Poly and I would travel around the streets of London with long-suffering Anne, in the search of an Italian restaurant. She was a woman of very fine tastes, but did not share our love of Italian food – nor our candid criticism of dishes that failed to come up to scratch.

Poor Anne would trail around the restaurants of Soho and its surrounding areas with Poly and I, acting like a pair of amateur critics with professional tastes. Each time pizza failed to appear on the menu, or to come up to expectations, I would stomp out muttering that the only thing to do was to set up my own pizzeria.

Poly and I felt rather alone in our love of Italian food. The Brits had never taken to the food – in 1903 pizza was famously described by food critic Lt-Col. Nathaniel Newnham-Davis as a "kind of Yorkshire pudding eaten with either cheese or anchovies in tomatoes flavoured with thyme". Outrageous!

Yet unfortunately this attitude prevailed throughout the United Kingdom, where pizza was treated as a novelty dish that nobody quite knew what to do with.

One evening, after we had been offered something that seemed to consist of three inches of dreary dough topped off by a thin sprinkling of indifferent cheese and a few sad olives, my face sported the usual disappointment at these pitiful attempts at making 'pizza'. What this country needed, I would lament, is a proper pizzeria that focused specifically (or, even better, solely) on making pizzas.

Anne, who may well have been slightly weary of these performances, seized her chance. She looked at me with a good-natured smirk and said, "You are always talking about it… for goodness sake, go and do it!"

So I did. Poly and Anne got married on 28 October 1965, and in the same autumn I entered into a partnership of my own that would last for a lifetime. Quite by chance, my housemate Sam Kiff had recently introduced me to a lady named Renée Brittain. As soon as we were acquainted, I was immediately enchanted by her. I never asked for Renée's age, but she was roughly 20 years my senior and had a long line of restaurants all over the Canary Islands.

Renée had stories that would make you howl with laughter, and her contact book was a who's who of the well-to-do. She was an awfully glamorous woman, even within the backdrop of cosmopolitan Soho. All in all, she was a great resource for any aspiring restaurateur in 1960s London.

Once Anne had planted that seed in my mind, I decided to approach Renée for some advice. As seems so often the case with successful people, she was eager to pass on tips of the trade to me. I can't stress how important she was in the eventual business' success.

Simply put, if it wasn't for Renée Brittain, there would be no PizzaExpress.

Her top tip was an obvious one – the most important thing is the quality of the food. If you ask 100 young children what makes a good restaurant, they will all say 'good food'. But if you put 100 adults in charge of making a restaurant good, they would list deals, advertising, brand management, paint schemes, seating plans... everything but the quality of the food.

You can advertise all you want... you can have the most beautiful restaurant... you can make your dishes the cheapest in town... but if the food is dreadful, it will not sell.

Italians have a phrase that fits Renée's mind-set perfectly, "A good restaurant needs no bush". The saying means that if the food is good enough, the restaurant doesn't need extravagant decorations. The food will sell itself. It became my mantra.

In the fast food business, it is easy to serve cheaply sourced food in a synthetic environment. Most favour low-cost ingredients and being slaves to keeping costs down. I never did. I stayed dedicated to quality and authenticity, preferring to maintain a high standard.

With this in mind, Renée and I started to scour the streets for inspiration. One night in the heart of Soho we finally came across a passable pizza. Although not a patch on what I had been privy to on the continent, it was the best I had eaten in England.

The pizza was served up in the Hostaria Romana restaurant in Dean Street, and I complimented the patron. However, he bashfully rejected the praise, acknowledging that it was not really like those you can taste in Italy and other counties in mainland Europe. It was then that he revealed the secret why pizzas in England were so rotten compared to mainland Europe... it's all about the ovens.

The patron, whose name I regrettably never knew, explained that it is impossible to cook good pizzas without a special oven. I asked why no one had ever imported such an oven from Italy. Someone had, he replied, but it had not been a success and the restaurant involved – the Romanella – had recently gone into liquidation.

He gave me directions to the restaurant, which was about 10 minutes' walk away, and said that if I hurried I might just pick up their oven cheaply. My eyes must have popped out of my head. I didn't wait until the next morning, I went over straight away. And I didn't walk there – I ran as fast as I could!

I begged the surprised owner to let me see his oven – and my excitement probably made him think he could etch the price up a few notches. He told me to follow him to the nearby warehouse to see this much recommended portal to Italian cuisine. We arrived in an old Pickfords' warehouse and he unveiled the object of my desires... which looked sad and old. And was beginning to rust.

As we inspected the sorry site behind the dirty tarpaulin cover, I couldn't imagine starting a multi-million dollar business with this forlorn looking cooker. Nevertheless, I trusted what the patron of the Hostaria Romana told me and thought I'd make an offer.

I said I would pay the Romanella £200 for the oven. Unfortunately, their valuation and mine were some way off, and the offer was rejected. I knew that my excitement had pushed the price up beyond this rust bucket's market value, and decided to cease negotiations.

But by now, I had the bit firmly between my teeth and knew I needed to get my hands on one of these traditional ovens if I wanted my pizzeria to be a success.

Two days later I was in Rome on a holiday, visiting old friends from my time there. I was determined not to let the matter drop. "Take me to your nearest pizzeria", I commanded the taxi driver, who promptly dropped me off at a little place near the Stazione Termini – doubtless musing on the forthright culinary demands of the English.

Once I arrived the proprietor informed me that he just ran an inelegant take-away shop with a variety of pizza I had never come across before. Sensing my disappointment, he told me there was a place miles away, on the outskirts of Rome where I could find Signor Notaro – a manufacturer of pizza ovens with the best reputation in the land.

So I hopped back into another taxi and went to see Sr Notaro. Within minutes of meeting, he had convinced me I was talking to a genius. A flamboyant man brimming with energy and ideas, he began excitedly sketching plans for a most flamboyant pizzeria in London while we were in conversation.

But first, I still needed that oven, and luckily Sr Notaro had numerous models that he was willing to sell. He showed them to me – all in pristine, perfect condition. They were a far cry from the vulgar one hiding under hiding under the decrepit sheet back in that London warehouse.

After a short chat, he said he would sell me it for £600 – including shipping and the transport costs for a man to teach us how to operate it. It seemed a fair deal, and within an hour of meeting Sr Notaro, I had bought my first oven. All I had to do now was create a restaurant that the oven could serve.

Back in London I began the arduous job of finding the correct ingredients to put into my pizza. I wanted to get the food right before I pushed onto looking for the location for the restaurant, in keeping with Renée's advice.

The essential cheese for pizza is mozzarella. I contacted the only authentic mozzarella maker in England – Carnevale, a company based in North London who were run by a fine man named Carmine Carnevale. I was so impressed after a visit to taste their product, I tied the manufacturer up for an exclusivity deal so that he could supply no rival restaurant. After all, I wanted PizzaExpress to be synonymous with their great cheese – not every other restaurant in London.

The trip to taste Carnevale's mozzarella led me, by remarkably good fortune, to the location of my restaurant. Their mozzarella maker was Margaret Zampi, the recently widowed partner of Mario Zampi, the film director. He died in 1963 – the same year that I came back to England – and his widow was now keen to sell his old failing pizza restaurant to a good successor.

Signor Zampi, who was born in Sora, Italy, had written and shot a number of zany comedies including *The Naked Truth* and *Too Many Cooks*. He was a big name, but even he had failed to make his London pizzeria a success. Sr Zampi shared my vision of launching pizza in England on a grand scale. No doubt because he, too, had experienced it in its proper form and knew the Brits would lap it up if given half a chance.

The restaurant was on Wardour Street – just off Oxford Street and a stone's throw from London's finest jazz club, Ronnie Scott's. Technically, it was the first ever PizzaExpress (although it was different in all but name to the restaurant I would go on to run).

Though ultimately unsuccessful, he had gone about the business in the right manner. First thing first – he imported a special oven. Sadly, it was electric, as he had thought authentic wood ovens would be prohibited, as the area was one of the capital's smokeless zones.

He also believed in a restaurant that focused on good food. Sr Zampi even set up a factory to provide the correct cheese. This was fior di latte – as near as he could come to true mozzarella in a country not blessed with wandering herds of buffalo.

In 1959, he had opened his first restaurant, hoping to attract his fellow movie stars there. Regrettably, they craved more luxurious food. Simple pizza was way ahead of its time and, thwarted, Sr Zampi turned the PizzaExpress into an ultra-elegant restaurant which was destined for success. It was just not the right fit for dynamic, cut-throat Soho.

But the location was perfect for my vision of high-quality, fast-made pizzas. So I bid to take it over. Eventually, the purchase set me back a total of £14,010… almost all being the cost of inheriting the old owners' debts.

Signora Zampi was most welcoming to the offer, and without persuasion agreed to sell me full ownership of PizzaExpress Ltd. I bought it for just £10. However, as well as taking the company's name, I also took on the rather more financially difficult task of repaying some £14,000 to their creditors.

My friends warned me it was a crazy deal – I was paying strangers' debts for something that I had never benefited from. But I was happy to inherit those debts if it meant I could acquire that endearing pizzeria. And so, Wardour Street in Soho was to be the location of my first restaurant.

Outside the Wardour Street branch in 1965 (left) and 2013 (right)

13
OUR FIRST MENU

I may have had no business plan other than my unwavering belief that good pizza would sell well. The only thing I wanted to sell at first was pizzas – which meant no dough balls, salads, desserts or pastas.

My abstinence from meat of course affected menu choices, and I also hoped that a vegetarian range of dishes may have been what set us apart from our competitors at the beginning. I did reluctantly decide to sell one meat dish, because I appreciated that the vast majority of our potential clients would be carnivores.

It is a strange moral quandary for a vegetarian restaurant proprietor: do you go against your personal instinct and serve meat, or go against your professional instinct and refuse it? Ultimately, I decided it would be foolish on both a personal and professional basis to absolutely deny the customer what they may want. Professionally, I realised it could lose PizzaExpress a lot of custom and personally I decided I didn't want to deny somebody of the freedom of choice. So I reluctantly put one meat dish on the menu.

All of our pizzas were made with 8oz of basic dough and 3oz of tomato. The pizza was served freshly baked and hot from the oven – and I am proud to say it was of a higher standard than any I had eaten in Britain.

Our first menu had 10 pizzas – all vegetarian except for one. I didn't call them 'vegetarian', as at the time that may have put people off. Vegetarianism today is synonymous with healthy eating, but back then it was a bit of an unknown culinary subculture. But if you say it's a mushroom pizza, people didn't seem to notice or remotely care that it did not satisfy their insatiable demand for meat.

All the mozzarella was sourced from a fine manufacturer called Carnevale, and their role in the success of my restaurant cannot be understated. It was (and still is) run by an Italian family, who import and distribute fresh food and drink products. Included in their range was the finest mozzarella imaginable – and that was one of the kicks that made PizzaExpress better than what had previously been passed off as 'pizza' in England, where clueless chefs used cheap cheese with a poor taste.

Here is the original 1965 menu – assume all pizzas have 8oz basic dough, 3oz tomato and 1.5oz mozzarella from Carnevale.

1. Pizza Margherita

Pizza Margherita is regarded as the generic flavour of the pizza family – almost like ready salted crisps. Margherita is the building blocks for any pizza; the stripped-down essentials.

It was always the first pizza listed on our menus, and always very popular. But what most people don't know about it is why it came to be regarded as the staple pizza – a story that dates back to a visit of Queen Margherita of Italy to Naples in 1889.

The locals served her a pizza resembling the colours of the Italian national flag – red (tomato), white (mozzarella) and green (basil). If I was to build a pizza empire, putting this on the top of the menu was a subtle nod to the industry forefathers who paved the way for people like me. So it was always the first dish on our menu.

2. Quattro Formaggi
— mozzarella, bel paese, edam/gouda, gruyere/emmental (1.5oz for each cheese)

Now known as 'Four Cheeses', I stuck with the Italian language for that veneer of authenticity.

To add interest, the cheeses were split into four separate quarters of the pizza. This allowed the pizzaiolo to add different herbs to different sections, such as chives on the ricotta, rosemary on the gruyere... and parsley anywhere.

In reality, any four cheeses can be chosen, but I decided upon ones that I felt both complemented each other, but also were noticeably different enough to make each section of the pizza noticeably different to the last.

3. Mushroom
— 3oz tomato, 2oz button mushrooms, garlic

The most important thing was not just to make sure that the mushrooms were thinly sliced, but also that they were absolutely bone dry. It is very easy to fall into what I call 'soggy mushroom syndrome'.

Mushrooms give off so much water that if they are not cut thinly and bone dry before being cooked, you will need to mop the pizza with a towel before serving.

4. Fiorentina
– *175g spinach leaves (washed), 1oz finely grated parmesan*

It was appropriate that such a good-looking pizza was named after one of Italy's most beautiful cities. Like most things from Florence, it was covered in spinach, which created a vivid green topping.

In other restaurants, the spinach can often be complemented with two or three medium-sized eggs. But I didn't want eggs on my menu – they look silly on a pizza, the smell is atrocious, and who wants a foetus for their tea?

5. Giardiniera
– *oregano, mixed vegetables, artichoke, olives, 1 desert spoon of grated Parmesan*

The earliest and most common feedback I ever received on this pizza was, "How on Earth do you pronounce it?"

While it may be hard for English people to say, it was damn sure worthy of a spot in my restaurant. Giardiniera pizzas are a real celebration of vegetables. Included in the dish was leaf spinach, sweet corn, chopped celery, peas, freshly sliced tomato, potato (boiled and sliced) and a thinly sliced onion. As you can imagine, it was a classic Italian vegetarian pizza, and merited a place on my menu.

Oh, and to answer the question, it's pronounced 'jar-dih-nair-ah'!

6. Pizza all'Andrea
— 60ml milk, 2tbsp extra virgin olive oil, 160g Ligurian olives, shaved parmesan and oregano leaves

Named after the famous Italian admiral Andrea Doria, this pizza was folded in half, and then folded once more. It was like a book in appearance, and its decreased size made it ideal for people who wanted to eat a pizza in a hurry.

7. Vegetarian
— for the dough: ½ teaspoon sea salt, ½ oz fresh eggs, ½ cup warm milk, teaspoon of oil. For the topping: large chopped onion, crushed garlic clove, 4 skinned and sliced tomatoes, 6 black olives, marjoram, 3oz thinly sliced vegetarian Cheddar cheese

Not the most creative of names, seeing as the majority of other dishes were also vegetarian, but it was one of the most creatively cooked pizzas we offered.

This was a pizza made to recommendations by the Vegetarian Society. It used wholemeal flour and had a different dough formula from previous recipes — a rather difficult pizza to make, but one that was delicious.

8. Pizza Olympico
— 2 spinach leaves, oregano, sambuca (or any other inflammable spirit), 2 coffee beans

This was an eye-catching and innovative pizza that had only recently been thought up. It was served in Amalfi, south-east Italy, to commemorate the Rome Olympic Games in 1960.

Once the pizza was cooked, it was taken from the oven and an egg-cup full of Sambuca was fixed firmly into its centre. The coffee beans were then added to the spirit and set on fire. The brave waiter then took the flaming pizza back to the table, creating an unforgettably spectacular sight to start off the meal.

9. Pizza Parmentier
– medium sized potato, rosemary, 1oz parmesan

This dish was named in honour of Antoine-Auguste Parmentier (1737-1813), who had popularised the previously scorned potato in France. Thanks to Parmentier's efforts, the Paris Faculty of Medicine declared potatoes edible in 1772 – helping to feed millions of hungry mouths.

Fittingly, potato featured prominently on the Pizza Parmentier. A medium sized potato was peeled into very thin slices no more than 1/8 inch thick. The slices were put on the tomato, sprinkled with salt, pepper and grated parmesan, and then baked for 20 minutes. Delicious!

10. American
– pepperoni, mozzarella, tomato

And finally, the controversial meat option.

My former American love Phyllis Senter had told me that her favourite pizza parlour in Florida covered the pizza with wafer-thin slices of pepperoni. Knowing that I was duty-bound to add a meat dish, I decided upon this one, and called it the 'American' due to this backstory.

As the man responsible for the restaurant, I always felt it was best to taste every dish. And therefore, due to this professional responsibility, I put my vegetarianism to one side and actually tried different sausages to go with the pizza. Although I didn't want to eat it, my reputation went along with the restaurant and I felt I was duty bound to sample every dish to make sure it was adequate for consumption by the general public.

I just about held my stomach for long enough to try four types of sausage: Hungarian gyula, Hungarian csabai, Polish kabanos and Spanish chorizos. None were to my taste, but I felt that Hungarian gyula complemented the pizza best, and so that was the sole item of flesh that made it onto the original PizzaExpress menu!

Over the course of time we added dozens more pizzas to the menu, often on rotation to keep the choices narrow in the Rustica tradition (which I shall come onto later). I still think the most interesting pizza we ever served up was the rather humorous 'Cockney Pride Pizza', which had three slices of chopped apple and three slices of chopped pear – 'apples and pears' being cockney rhyming slang for 'stairs'. Sadly, it wasn't to last long and it didn't prove to be one of our more popular pizzas – something that doesn't surprise many when I tell them of the ingredients today.

Of course, we also needed chefs to make the pizzas and waiters to serve them. I decided that it would be a good idea to install a black-and-white horizontally striped uniform, like the ones I had seen that talented pizzaiolo Benito sport back in Forte dei Marmi.

I felt at the time it was an instantly iconic look, and hoped that dressing our staff in the same way would add a touch of Italian authenticity to the company – a little touch that could go a long way.

14
TURNING THE DREAM
INTO REALITY

I did a deal with a fine Italian chef from Ventimigilia to become our first manager. His name was Gino Plato, and he came with years of valuable experience in restaurants in both Italy and England.

With a manager and menu in place, now we needed to get the building up and running to become a serviceable restaurant. Armed with a sadly inefficient array of tools and paintbrushes, but with the compensation of plenty of enthusiasm, we started to desecrate the interior of the site.

The demolition crew was myself, good old Poly and some pals from the City. The bar proved particularly difficult to break down, and one morning we hailed three hefty passers-by to help us push over that strongly built shrine to Bacchus. Never a lesser equipped team of labourers will you ever see!

I was afraid that when my special oven arrived from Rome that it would simply tumble through the old Soho floor. It weighed one ton, and those floorboards looked like they would tremble at its mere sight – and so we had a great game locating and fixing a steel beam to support the floorboards. We did so with the capable help of an amiable Jamaican chap who was working on the Swiss Centre building site on the other side of the road. When the oven finally arrived it falling through the floor became the least of my worries… because we couldn't get the giant thing through the blasted door!

There was only one thing for it – we'd have to knock the wall down. So we took to our hammers and knocked a hole in the wall large enough to navigate the one-ton oven through. I shall never forget the resulting sight of Poly, the Earl of Norbury, stood in full dinner suit as he navigated it through the dusty aftermath of the brand new hole in my brand new restaurant.

A good restaurant may need no bush, but it cannot serve good food without a good oven. Knocking the wall down was a small price to pay to make sure London's newest diner was equipped to serve up food unlike any that had graced the capital before!

It was obvious that my intention was not properly understood by Soho's natives. After weeks of painting, pulling and preparing, the restaurant was still not open. One old gent strongly advised me to sell sandwiches to cover the rent. The general consensus was that pizza would, as it had before, fail to capture any interest in Britain.

But I knew what they didn't – that an authentic, Italian oven would make my food unlike the 'pizza' they were comparing my future product to. The resolve of knowing how I had loved real pizza while on the continent gave me the strength to ignore people who urged me to sell chips with the pizza.

Nothing could be further from my mind. However, that idea did capture somebody's imagination. Before I'd even opened up, a competitor had arrived on Wardour Street.

Dikko Bar, owned by Bozo Ivanovic (a fellow Cambridge graduate), set up in the shop next door. Bozo used a cleverly thought-out American idea – baking frozen pizza which was sold by the site. I believe my hand-crafted pizza was a better quality, and the fact you are

reading Boizot's book and not Bozo's may be an indication
that I was right.

I say this partly in jest, as the two of us became good
friends over the years. Although the Dikko Bar wasn't
quite as successful as PizzaExpress, Bozo Ivanovic must be
remembered as one of the country's true pizza pioneers.

I shall go into some detail about that first restaurant
on Wardour Street. It was the blueprint for all that
came afterwards, and I think getting to know how that
pizzeria operated is an integral part to understanding the
PizzaExpress story.

One tip that I had for the layout came from Sr Notaro,
who recommended that I base it on a specific kind of
Italian establishment known as a Pizza Rustica. Dishes
were delivered quickly, because a narrow menu meant
food could be prepared long in advance, and then waited
to be ordered and then promptly served up to the hungry
customer. With a larger menu, it would not make sense to
cook meals before they were ordered, as how could you
tell which options would interest the customer that day?

In Rome, these Pizza Rusticas are as common as our
fish-and-chip shops. However, they were also as out of
place in London as a cockney chippy would be in Turin.
In Italy, children call into Pizza Rusticas on their way to
school in the mornings. They collect a small slab of pizza
which they use to form a sandwich with a chocolate bar –
using Nutella as a filling. Yes, sounds awful to me too! We
didn't take it that far, but we did implement the concept of
a fast-paced restaurant.

Gino Plato taught me how to make the dough to feed
the oven. I was keen to be a hands-on manager, and
would help prepare the dishes with the help of Gaetana, a

splendid grey-haired Sicilian lady. She spoke little English so we chatted in Italian.

The location was a four-storey, terraced building at 29 Wardour Street. I bought one of the offices above the restaurant, which meant the creaky stairs became something of a rabbit run. The downstairs was between a restaurant named Garners and Regent Boutique, a clothes store with pretty dresses in the window. Between us and Garners was an alleyway, which helped us wheel out our waste.

Our building did not stand out on the road, so we had to do what we could to make it memorable. I wanted it to be a highly neon-lit pizzeria. I wanted it to stand out as the super hygienic building in the midst of a notoriously run-down street.

We had two large windows either side of the entrance door – a perfect way to advertise our product. I had brought the dough mixer into the front part of the window so passers-by could see one of our chefs, Gaetana, making the dough. We rolled it out on a big slab of marble because customers to watch it rise in front of their own eyes. The open kitchen would prove to be a valuable unique selling point for the restaurant.

At the back of the cooking area was the infamous oven, meaning the dishes would be completed from start to finish in front of the customer. Preparing the food in this public setting proved to be a popular idea. I suppose it dispels any hygiene fears, but really I think the benefit is it adds the diner to the culinary experience. When you see the dough being made, the toppings prepared and even the flames of the oven, you really feel a part of the whole food making experience.

In my first blueprint, I had wanted people to either leave carrying their slices, or stay in the restaurant and eat it standing up. This is the way they do it in Pizza Rusticas in Rome and Milan, but every single person I proposed the idea to in England to thought I was mad. I suppose they were wise, as now such a place conjures up thoughts of these smaller takeaway shops that now dominate moonlit High Streets.

And so, before opening, I eventually agreed to take my friends' advice, and installed five tables – they weren't ordinary tables though, they were made of fine marble. That was enough to seat 20 people, but still presented the option to walk back out the door with your order in a takeaway box.

Although I was prepared to relent on the tables, there was one thing I was stubborn enough to maintain that there should be no washing up. Customers would be served their pizza slices on disposable plates. They would eat with plastic knives and forks, and sip their coffee from paper cups. I thought this tied in with the 'fast food' mantra, and also saved time and resources in washing up. The customer would finish their meal, and we would simply throw the dirty paper plates out.

Controversially, I also decided not to sell pizza in the traditional circular shape. Instead, our pizza was moulded in rectangular trays. I would spread out the dough, tomato and cheese using a rolling pin, then cut it up into eight oblongs sell it on a greaseproof paper for two shillings a slice.

The reason for this was not driven by a dream to change the way pizza was sold, I just thought at first it would take off more as a 'snack' than a 'meal'. A rectangle was easier to divide into transportable oblong slices, whereas a circular pizza would be cut into less convenient triangles with a curved edge.

D-Day (as I referred to the restaurant's launch date) was Saturday, 27 March, 1965. With the big day fast approaching, I hit another snag. My first manager quit. That's right – he walked away from PizzaExpress just before we even opened!

Gino had agreed to help with the preliminary work that needed to be done to get us up and running. In my optimism, I had supposed there would be very little for him to do. I was hopelessly wrong.

While Gino was prepared to help out a bit, as the date came closer and the manual workload continued to grow, he walked out on me. He was crestfallen and apologetic – an absolute gentleman – when he said he didn't feel the workload fitted with his professional ambition. Apparently, scraping painted names off glass windows was not his cup of espresso.

I was upset but I couldn't blame him – I had sold the position on what I expected it to be rather than what it turned out to be. So I was delighted that Gino went on to run one of the best Italian restaurants in London, The Imperia. But his resignation seemed to be contagious, and soon my already small team was reduced even further. Gianni Giochi, my imported pizzaiolo, promptly announced that he too would be leaving. He had fulfilled his duty of showing us how to operate the oven, and was heading back to Rome.

But still, no rest for the wicked. Poly, Renée and I continued to feverishly carry out the fitting, with home-made counters devised from Dexion and hessian. There were hastily converted tables and DIY tiling. It was looking rough and ready, but somehow we got it ready to open by D-Day.

Before he went back home, Gianni gave me one final tip. He said that whenever a new pizzeria opened, they would give away their pizzas for free. I pride myself in the fact that PizzaExpress has never resorted to 'Buy One, Get One Free' or 'Kids Eat For Half Price' deals – but I did make it a tradition to give away free pizzas whenever a new restaurant opened.

The reason for this was not as philanthropic as our potential future customers thought. The real reason Italian chefs did this was because before charging for a pizza, they had to test the oven and the dough on the backs of the customers.

15
'D-DAY'

I had absolute confidence that we were onto a winner when we arrived for the first day of trading that Saturday, in late March 1965. That feeling intensified at noon, when we opened our doors to a huge crowd that snaked off into the Soho horizon. The rumour of free food was rare in London, and it had seemingly spread like wildfire throughout the capital.

We were greeted by the resplendent sight of crowds of Sohoites, who seemed to hold out three hands for free pizza (and take a fourth slice for their pal who couldn't make it out of the office). We handed out hundreds of free slices, and the opening day completed its two objectives – creating a buzz and proving our pizza was better than others in London.

After the first day's 'trading' (or rather 'giving'), prices were introduced. We charged a very reasonable two bob a slice, but sadly even that was enough to see our trade taper off considerably. But the trade we did have was regular and full of praise for the product. I was sure that word-of-mouth would eventually help sales increase. As ever, the principle of the food selling itself stayed strong.

As I had hoped, the customers did enjoy watching Gaetana and I making the dough in the restaurant in front of them – a tradition that remains in PizzaExpress restaurants to this day. I'm not sure if it's because they can trust the pizzaiolo isn't sneezing in the dough, but customers responded well to the all-inclusive nature of our service.

Our opening hours were dictated by the cash till, not the clock. It drives me mad when you see a restaurant turn away business, as PizzaExpress does now in the minutes before the restaurants close at 11pm sharp. I suppose once a business gets bigger it has to give up a sense of autonomy and become more regulated. But that original PizzaExpress was very much an autonomous ship – and a fun one to be a crew member.

Today if you're coming out of a show at 10.30pm you have to rush to a PizzaExpress to get served before the 11pm closing time. Back in those days, hours did not matter and at the weekends we stayed open until four or five in the morning if there were customers. The staff would mingle with diners, singing and dancing around our speakers as they belted out some jazz music or the latest Beatles hit.

The cosmopolitan population of Soho, which ranged from middle-eastern street brawlers to middle-England dukes, created an almost fairground atmosphere. But sadly, the takings at first were not great – probably because we were selling for too cheap a price. But I was still sure that once it caught on, the prices were sustainable – we just needed to sell more of them.

In our restaurants, the Italian image was very prominent and deliberately cultivated. Few concessions were made to English traditions; we were an Italian restaurant and handled ourselves as such. Our staff were mainly Italian – although later on we were to become like the League of Nations (something I regard with immense pride).

In the Wardour Street restaurant, I loved shouting at the staff like a true Italian, and with most of the staff coming from the Old Boot I chose to speak their language.

Apparently I was so authentic the customers actually thought my Peterborough background was a fabrication.

Without a little knowledge of Italian, the enterprise would have failed. Without the language, I would never have been able to communicate with the staff. Today, people all around the globe watch English language television and listen to British and American music, but back then very few Italians could speak English.

Soon after opening, I gave a job to a new 27-year-old pizzaiolo from Naples named Rino Silvestri. One evening, I received a phone call from an immigration officer based in Dover. He said he had intercepted a Neapolitan, who spoke no English at all. All he had was a scrap of paper with my name, and the restaurant's phone number. Somehow, they had bridged the linguistic gap to deduce that he was a plumber – and immediately phoned me to ask why I had hired a plumber from Italy rather than Islington.

The voice at the other end of the line told me they were about to return him to Italy. "No, no!", I cried. "He is here to make pizza. Even if a plumber by trade, he is also a Neapolitan and all Neapolitans know about pizza – just as a cockney from Bow knows about fish-and-chips!"

I am pleased to say they let him pass into the country, and Rino became our star pizzaiolo, a highly successful manager and eventually a franchisee.

Within weeks of opening, I ran into my old Cambridge friend, Ronald Simson, who came into the restaurant quite by chance as a customer. I hadn't seen Ron in years, but we quickly hit it off again – and he promptly gave me some blunt home truths about improvements he thought I could make.

While I tried to explain that 'a good restaurant needs no bush', he had reservations that people wouldn't want to eat using plastic knives and forks. After all, who wants to see their piping hot pizza served with plastic cutlery melting under its bubbling cheese?

The lack of cutlery had puzzled customers, and it similarly failed to impress Ron. Wisely, he urged me to trade up a little – and soon we were trading from the best Woolworths china and silver.

He also had criticisms for selling pizza in rectangular slices. He bluntly said, "Peter, I think you are mad not to sell it in a circle", so I decided to change the approach. We would still make the dough in the same way, but just in a circle and put it in a round dish.

After those two tweaks were made, our takings started to climb. I'll grudgingly admit that in this occasion, the restaurant needed a bit of a bush, but once inside – the customers were ours. They became almost instantly loyal, and those initial years of PizzaExpress were reliant on return business from our first diners and their endorsements to friends. We had no advertising budget, after all!

As customers grew, I started to reap ever-improving profits. I proudly showed this steady upward climb during many an eyeball-to-eyeball confrontation with creditors who still harboured their doubts. I was delighted to be able to reward the patient ones who kept my account, and saw their investments grow through the years.

Another major boost was given to the company after I decided to import Peroni Nastro Azzurro to the restaurant. I was the first person to ever order a case to the

UK, which is quite astounding as it is now apparently in the top 10 list for most sold beers in the country.

Peroni was one of the many beers I had fallen in love with while in Italy. I decided to import it to the UK to be sold in my restaurant, although it had absolutely zero brand recognition at the time. But it was one of the best-selling pale lagers in Italy. I was thoroughly confident that it would complement our Italian cuisine perfectly.

The first consignment arrived at a depot in Camden, and we employed several old lags from the nearby hostel to unload it. Somewhat disastrously, several cases were dropped – but they didn't go to waste. The contents were mopped up and consumed on the spot through the broken bottles by our helpers… how considerate of them!

I wanted the exclusive rights to sell Peroni in the UK (a concession), and went out to Naples to try to negotiate this with Dr Spadaccio, their sales director. Unfortunately, there was a lock-out at the brewery and I spent a few agreeable days in Capri whilst this was sorted out.

We never got that concession, meaning that although we had brought Peroni to the country, once the secret got out every Tom, Dick and Harry was able to sell it as well.

I still believe the boost that Peroni gave to PizzaExpress helped us to get off the ground, and certainly made me a rich man. It is now one of Britain's leading imported beers, and is available in most pubs, bars and restaurants in the country. I think for this reason, people are often surprised when I tell them that the first place to unleash it upon the British public was PizzaExpress.

While I was in Naples courting the Peroni deal, I also stumbled upon a fantastic deal that set us up with a fantastic wine supplier. While on a beach, a small child ran out in front of me and I tripped over her. The next thing I knew, a very officious-looking man came and asked me what had happened. I explained that it was an accident and neither of us seemed to be hurt, and so nothing further should be made of the incident.

However, the man told me that the girl was a member of the Frescobaldi family – a prominent Florentine Noble family who had helped to mould Tuscany.

While all of this was unfolding, the girl's father came over and seemed keen to calm the whole situation down. He asked me why I was in Naples, and I explained that I was an English restaurateur looking for drinks to add to my menu.

The gentleman confirmed that he was from the Frescobaldi family, and that they had previously exported their Marchesi de Frescobaldi wine to King Henry VIII. Within minutes, we were setting up a business deal that would bring their wine back to Britain and allow the people of England to drink their fantastic wine for decades to come. All because I almost fell over a small child!

I don't think the deal would have come about without my years of international salesman, but there was also a magical combination of luck, fate and co-incidence. It all resulted in a strong trade deal and a magnificent wine being added to our menu.

16
HOW TO MAKE THE PERFECT PIZZA

I can't tell you how many dinner parties I have gone to where the host wants to make a homemade pizza to impress me. Of course, I would always smile and compliment them upon finishing it, but they made so many mistakes.

The key is simple: use the correct equipment.

I always believe our success came predominantly from the kitchen. The quality of food on offer was so high, so it makes sense to take a step away from the business chronology to give tips into making the perfect pizza.

It is a case of 'clear the decks' when you are going to make a pizza, and the more uncluttered space you can give yourself to work on, the better. Ideally, pizza should be cooked in an oven at 370°C (700°F), heated from both the top and the bottom. Without this sort of furnace, the dough is not thoroughly cooked and appears disproportionately heated – and often burnt.

One consolation of using an inferior oven is that it is easier to eat with your fingers when it is crispy. But one thing that I will never abide is cooking a pizza in a microwave – unless you like eating a soggy embarrassment of a pizza that will crumble in your hands. Wood ovens produce the best pizza (as the padrone of the old Gioia Mia pizzeria in Rome said, a wood oven is the 'anima della pizza' – the pizza's very soul). Sadly, they are not domestic to Britain, and that has created many problems in my search to serve the perfect pizza.

In terms of the working surface, cool marble is best. I feel that baking trays or pans are important too, even though Neapolitan pizzaiolos do not use them. You can copy them if you wish, but the whole process considerably trickier. What you will certainly need is a large peel or paddle to slide the pizza in and out of the oven – ideally an oven with a stone heart if possible.

One of the major flaws amateur pizzaiolos perpetually make comes with the dough. Don't worry that your dough will be too thick – thickness will not kill a pizza as long as the dough is light and airy. However, thinness will kill a pizza... and it often does.

You must always pinch a rim in the dough so that the filling does not spill over into the cooking. I suggest you use 8oz of flour in most of the dough recipes – because that would be enough for two pizzas. You can always freeze the dough after it has been kneaded. Then you can have a quick pizza a few days later within 15 minutes – just put it in a hot oven for 15 minutes.

At home, I recommend you lower the circle of dough into a round 9 inch pan, with sloping edges not more than 1.5 inches high. That will give you a pan of about 10 inches across the top –traditional dimensions for a circular pizza. A pizza of this size will feed one hungry person, or two as a light bite. Of course, if you are making pizzas from scratch, you need not cater to the usual circular shape, and pizzas are just as tasty oblong or square as they are circular.

Pizza is a substantial food. The dough base is filling enough – so when topping it, you should avoid any further ingredients which would overdo the starch content. You can use flour-based sauces, potatoes, or even beans on pizza – it does not unbalance the dish.

You must not overfill a pizza. I have sometimes been carried away when topping an uncooked pizza in one of my experimental sessions – it begins to look amazingly attractive, another olive here, and a little more cheese there. Remember though that the dough will expand a little when it starts to cook, cheese melts and bubbles – and before you know where you are, the whole thing has over-flowed in the oven and is unpalatable.

CHAPTER IV:
THE BUSINESS EXPANDS

Once the pizza is in the oven, the bread will expand rapidly. It is vitally important that you monitor the pizza to ensure the crust is not crumbling apart in the oven – that would ruin the dish.

Similarly when a business grows, its manager has to oversee the expansion and ensure that the whole thing does not become out of control. But as long as you monitor carefully and enforce barriers to stop problems, you should encourage as much growth as possible.

17
ADDING PEARLS TO
THE NECKLACE

As the company started to become more and more popular, we decided that expansion was the next logical step in the business model. In 1967, we opened a second branch, less than a mile away in Coptic Street, in the Camden borough of London. The site was in kicking distance of the British Museum, and I figured there would always be a hungry flock of culture vultures.

The décor for that second restaurant was designed by a true master of the craft named Enzo Apicella, with a little help from his artistic friends and inspiration drawn from a few crates of whisky. But it was Enzo who was the true visionary behind the physical walls that held every future PizzaExpress – and he would go on to become a dear friend.

His design for the restaurant was absolutely brimming with personal touches – such as gigantic green plants and spotlights, and original murals of recipes from Ancient Rome. His fresh, colourful interiors were a perfect complement to the pizza and the incoming wave of Italian food.

Enzo and I always had a tumultuous relationship. We did not always part on good terms but we remained in partnership for many years and are still friends. I just put the squabbles down to that fiery Italian temperament.

Coptic Street proved to be the first of a long line of restaurants designed by him all over the world – including the Terrazza in Venice and the Meridiana in Brompton Road, Knightsbridge. His restaurants were always effortlessly trendy while also being functional. They were also designed to be noisy and incredibly sociable.

Enjoying a pizza in 2013 with my dear friend Enzo Apicella

One humorous element he implemented that I never took on was Enzo's decision to place a life-size papier-mâché version of himself at a good table by the door in the Meridiana. It almost looked like a Guy Fawkes doll. I'm not sure if it was there to attract customers or just illustrate Enzo's ownership, but I didn't dare follow suit. I was always afraid that a likeness of me in a PizzaExpress could act more like a scarecrow scaring people away from my restaurants!

I knew the pizzas in Coptic Street would sell just as they had in Wardour Street, but by now had conceded the setting had to be right to first attract people inside. I wanted to create something iconic, a brand that people would instantly recognise as 'PizzaExpress'.

I immediately tasked Enzo with the job of refurbishing the building, which was an old dairy. I wanted him to turn it into something with a bit of pizzazz befitting my vision for PizzaExpress. However, whenever I asked what he was planning, Enzo's Neapolitan hackles rose and he would abruptly tell me not to worry, and leave it in his hands. I never took these passionate outbursts personally and left Enzo to get on with his job. Enzo's sense of self-belief was contagious, and I trusted him implicitly.

The result was a fast, casual-style restaurant. The focal point was a large Neapolitan-style counter, behind which the pizzas were made and the customers could chat with the pizzaiolos. He added sweeping green paint to the ceiling and a smattering of lamps on the table. It was a minimalist triumph, and drew much praise from the visitors.

Upon entering the restaurant, the customer would come into what we called the 'Living Lab'. The distinctive design, although never exactly replicated, is now synonymous with PizzaExpress establishments.

In the middle of the floor space was a big bright red counter, behind which pizzaiolos would work like beavers to toss pizzas high into the air right in front of the customer. The counter was built by two South African men from a marble slab and had been painted brick red.

Enzo had the fantastic idea of extending it all around the seating area. The walls of the counter snaked like a river through the building. The flowing red walls served as dividers between the tables. It was just private enough so each table had an intimate feeling, but not secluded or cut off from the majority of the restaurant. The design also expertly cut off space in the restaurant, making it less obvious when we weren't full.

The tables themselves were circular, and were littered with devices to aid with acoustics. This was because I wanted the restaurant to sound alive, and also because I dreamt of adding live jazz music to our 'menu'.

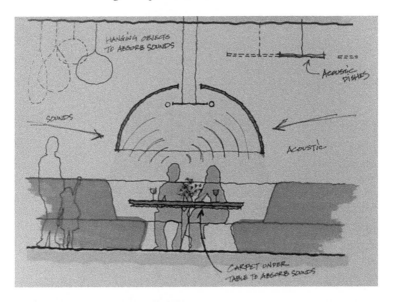

To absorb the sounds, we put carpet under the table and hung domes from the ceilings. Large LED domes with the phrase 'Serve Me' were put over each table – ostensibly pop art, but also functional because they did a job of rebounding those sound waves to make clean noise. For the same reason, a thin layer of carpet was placed under the tables.

Enzo also attached 'acoustic dishes' to the ceiling – they looked like a fleet of UFOs attached to the ceiling by a piece of string, but they did the job and made sound echo around each table like a bat cave.

However, perhaps the most iconic thing about that second restaurant was created not by Enzo, but rather by a talented American artist named Nancy Fouts. She had been recommended to me by a friend, and I tasked her with the all-important responsibility of creating a new logo, which would hang over the entrance.

Nancy did a fantastic job; it was everything you could want from a company logo – memorable, identifiable and synonymous with the business. It was a pizza-shaped circle, with the words 'PizzaExpress' written in a bold font. Around the words were red, white and green squiggles – representing Italy as well as tomato, bread and vegetables all at once. I immediately fell in love with the simple yet effective emblem.

Although the colours are now white and dark blue, the design itself has never changed. Thousands, if not millions, of casual diners have seen the logo and been persuaded to head into a PizzaExpress for a meal. It was instantly recognisable, and became a tremendous marketing tool that was perfect for our brand.

With our authentic pizzas and Enzo's excellent design, the Coptic Street branch prospered. The manager there was Patrice Brun, and he pulled in huge takings each week. And from such humble beginnings, an empire was formed.

After Wardour Street and Coptic Street, we added a third restaurant in Fulham Road, Chelsea, beneath prominent '60s mod fashion designer Mary Quant's old workrooms.

Again, Enzo designed the layout in a simple, 'pop art' manner – but the original design was not accepted by the Chelsea Council. The main bone of contention was the now iconic' 'PizzaPizzaPizzaPizzaPizzaPizzaPizza' sign around the sides of the restaurant. Enzo or I were both too stubborn to alter the design.

I had to appeal to the Minister of Town and Country Planning, armed with 300 letters of support signed by customers. Thankfully, the governmental bureaucrats overruled the local authority bureaucrats, and the neon sign remained. It soon became our unofficial badge and nickname of the company – 'PizzaPizza'.

For those first three restaurants, I was very much still actively involved. I hired managers, but they were definitely all 'Peter Boizot' restaurants. But I realised that, having expanded from one to three branches in a couple of years, there was nothing saying we wouldn't be able to grow even further. However, with increased growth I recognised that I would have to entrust the running of the restaurants down to managers more and more.

The ability for PizzaExpress to expand came thanks to other investors buying into my vision of High Street pizza shops. I sold people the right to trade under the PizzaExpress banner. In return for using our successful business model, they would kick up a percentage of the profits back to me. This meant that the model could spread not just to Soho High Streets, but all over London (and hopefully, the world).

We operated a franchisee model before the word really existed. I gave good people the chance to run the restaurants and they would pay money back to the company. I was proud to be a job creator – for each restaurant there would be a franchisee and a staff of around 12. A lot of people made a lot of money from those restaurants, myself included.

The people who bought franchises were, thankfully, all excellent people and we never had problems with certain wings dragging down the name of PizzaExpress. Many of them came from within the company – solid workers who had cut their teeth and wanted to run their own restaurant.

Fittingly, the first franchisee came from that mould. Mario Molino, who came to work in PizzaExpress on Dean Street, became the first person to buy a branch, in Gloucester Road, Kensington. Mario was a fantastic person to be our first franchisee – charming and hard-working, if a little too much so at times.

He was a demanding man, and held his employees to the highest of standards. But most importantly, he was a man we could trust.

After Gloucester Road came branches in two South London areas – Streatham and Wimbledon. Unlike Gloucester Road, they were not franchises but branches being run by the head office (that is, to say, they were being run by me).

Some friends asked if this was getting away from the artisan brand PizzaExpress had built up in swashbuckling Soho and the swinging West End, as

Streatham and Wimbledon were more downmarket areas than the bohemian chic spots that housed our other PizzaExpress restaurants.

Streatham had once had the longest High Street in the capital, and even been described as the 'West End of South London'. But post-war decline had seen grotesque new housing blocks and bingo halls built, and residents had steadily moved away. The war had an even more devastating effect on Wimbledon – many of the buildings had been damaged by bombing and the area now failed to compete with neighbouring Kingston and Sutton.

The pessimists thought selling a franchise to such areas could diminish the PizzaExpress brand, but I paid little attention to such a negative viewpoint. Firstly, and most importantly, pizza was a dish from Naples – a city with far more social problems than Wimbledon or Streatham. And secondly, if things were as bad as purported in those boroughs, wouldn't it be fantastic to bring our great culinary experience to its people?

And so, branches were opened in those boroughs. I had little to do with the running of those restaurants, but I would always attend the opening parties and make the franchisees know that, if they needed it, help was only a telephone call away.

By this stage, each restaurant was bringing in the cash and franchisees were lining up to take on a branch. By the end of the decade, there were six PizzaExpress restaurants in Wardour Street, Coptic Street, Chelsea, Kensington, Streatham and Wimbledon – we were expanding faster than our loyal customers' belt buckles.

However, there was also one rogue 'branch' in operation... without my knowledge.

To my utter bemusement, a friend who had just been to Athens gave me a telephone call to congratulate me on our expansion to Greece. He told me that the PizzaExpress there is buzzing, full every night. This was a lovely thing to hear, but there was one problem – I had never been asked for permission to open a restaurant there!

After some digging, I learnt that the phoney 'PizzaExpress' was being run by a former waiter at our Wardour Street branch. He was a Greek chap who thought it would be a good idea to take the business model and go home with it – and that's what he did! Everything from the menu to the uniforms and even the logo were those being used by us. He even used our sugar sachets and napkins, which I assume he had taken from Wardour Street.

My reaction to this news surprised my close friends. I was delighted! Seemingly, the principles I had put in place had been a success in Greece, where they are more used to 'properly' made pizzas than in England. I was always paranoid that our food was not *quite* up to authentic standards, so to hear that a busy PizzaExpress clone was actually a rather well-received validation of our brand.

Still, I realised it was a risky business. There was nothing to stop this Grecian Peter Boizot-wannabe to cut costs on pot washing, and then the whole restaurant has food poisoning… and then my PizzaExpress unfairly gets a bad name.

I asked our lawyers to look into what we could do about stopping this rogue PizzaExpress franchise, and was disappointed to hear that our copyright was apparently difficult to enforce in Greece. There was nothing we could do to stop him. The only solace I had is that our Greek imitator received none of the help from the parent company which our official franchisees benefited from – but other than that, he continued to trade.

However, it wasn't all headaches. In 1970, something fantastic happened that would change PizzaExpress forever for the better – a man by the name of Eddie Kidney joined our ranks. I want to break from the chronology of my life story when talking about Eddie, because his career with PizzaExpress teaches a good lesson in how we managed to expand as a company.

In any business that employs good people, the sum of its parts can make the company as a whole stronger. The expression of 'big fish in a little pond' makes no sense at all – that big fish should be able to help you to make your pond bigger.

Eddie joined as a skinny 22-year-old American who was passing through London on a gap year. He joined the PizzaExpress in Fulham Road as a washer-up, and soon afterwards found a good woman and ended up staying for longer than he bargained for.

He is a fantastic example of the breaks the restaurant offered its employees – and how well it rewarded those who committed to taking those breaks. I met Eddie soon after he came to the Fulham Road branch, and knew after we spoke for the first time that he wouldn't be a pot-washer for life.

Eddie tells me there is one thing I said that made an impression on him when he was a young man – that "work should never be a chore". I believe I was talking to Fay Maschler, the Evening Standard's food critic, but Eddie claims that idea planted the seed in his head that he could smile and enjoy himself at work.

That, combined with his abilities, made him a perfect employee.

Some people say that I have been harsh on my employees, and I was known to tell them of things they were doing wrong in front of the paying public. But I never meant it maliciously, and I hoped that it meant they would not make the same mistake again.

But Eddie never made any mistakes. He was rapidly promoted from pot washer to waiter, and then onto cashier. Before long, a spot opened up as assistant manager and then (in the same year) he was made the branch's manager. Before he was 30, Eddie had been made the general manager of PizzaExpress, a job he held between 1979 and 1985, when he stayed with the company but moved away from the head office and back into the restaurants.

Thanks to being given the opportunity to grow within the company, Eddie helped us to expand as well. As a consequence, this 22-year-old American boy wound up staying in England for the rest of his life – with the majority of it being spent working for me. Eddie was not my only fantastic employee, but his story shows what I believe to be my key business skill – the ability to identify talent and then utilise as much as possible.

I also kept an open ear to suggestions my colleagues had – including adding Dough Balls to the menu. I am not, and never have been, a big fan of the starter, which simply sees 16 dollops of bite-sized chunks of baked pizza dough along with a garlic, butter and olive oil dip. They were simple, and to me uninteresting, but I agreed to put them onto our menu in 1970 and they proved to be an extremely popular addition. They have now been served at PizzaExpress for over four decades.

This open sharing and implementing of ideas serves as a benefit to both employees and the company. It seems obvious to me, and I think any successful businessman has to have an open mind for other peoples' good ideas.

My key message to anybody stuck in what they perceive to be a dead-end job is that enthusiasm and competence will get your boss' attention, and you will get out of that situation far quicker than you imagine.

However, enthusiasm without competence will keep you in that rut – as will competency without enthusiasm.

18
MIXING PIZZA AND JAZZ

In addition to Eddie joining the company in 1970, there was another change: jazz was introduced to our restaurants.

I moved into a spacious one-bedroom flat in Dean Street – directly opposite the PizzaExpress in Wardour Street. This flat also doubled as my office; I suppose I couldn't bear to be away from my work! With the restaurant opposite me and a never-ending stream of letters coming through my letterbox, this gave me an excellent base not only for the business but also to explore Soho in the rare times I was not working.

The London jazz scene was thriving at the time, and my new base was less than 100 yards from Ronnie Scott's, on 47 Frith Street, and little further from the 100 Club, on 100 Oxford Street. Ronnie's was my favourite place to go. Now it's one of the oldest jazz clubs in the world, but back then it was the most vibrant upstart venue in the capital. They would have all the popular names coming through, as well as a seemingly never-ending supply of young guns trying to make an impact on the industry.

I would rarely make a booking at Ronnie Scott's, but due to being an increasingly well-known face in the area, I would often be privileged enough to get priority seating around the stage. Most importantly, that came with table service, so I wouldn't have to queue with my back to the stage for a top-up while the act was on stage.

The place was named after its charismatic owner. Ronnie, like me, was an Englishman who went abroad and came back home inspired by what he had seen. I got to know him fairly well. Ronnie would say that he went touring America in the 1940s after being taught to play the tenor saxophone by Vera Lynn's father-in-law, but I was never sure if that was a joke or the truth.

After returning to England, he set up his eponymous club just in time for the 1960s culture boom in central London. The venue opened in a Gerrard Street basement in October 1959, before the larger space on Frith Street opened in 1965.

Ronnie was a real character, at home with celebrities as much as the everyday punter. I recall him telling me in 1968 that he had been in the studio with some band recording a song, but that he doubted anybody would ever hear it. A few months later, I heard through a mutual friend that the song in question was Lady Madonna by The Beatles – and Ronnie had played the saxophone solo! He had downplayed performing with the biggest pop band of all time, and he must have known it would be a hit – with his bridge being a focal point of it.

Despite being a show-man, Ronnie was not a show-off. I respected that, and it certainly made a large impact on the way I presented myself professionally.

The jazz artists he booked were mainly American, as that's where the scene was and always will be hottest. They would come for stints as short as a couple of days to as long as a month. You would get the likes of Wes Montgomery and Ben Webster, but also English musicians like Tubby Hayes. These were huge names, a real coup to book for a live performance.

Meanwhile, my restaurant branches continued to pop up like mushrooms in a cow pasture, I started to get rather competitive with how the old branches were doing compared to the new. I am a firm believer that competition drives businesses forward, and it's a wonderful thing to be competitive against your own company.

I wanted to do something to make the old branches stand out. To do this, I drew inspiration from my experiences past and present.

Ever since my days eating pizza in Germany, I had been enamoured with the idea of jazz playing while people ate. In Bavaria the music came from a jukebox, and in PizzaExpress it was coming from speakers. This did a good job of setting a pleasant ambience – but those weren't the adjectives I was hoping people would use to describe the PizzaExpress experience. I wanted it to be a real night out.

That was the sort of energy you could get at Ronnie Scott's. So the decision was obvious – marry up pizza eating to listening to live jazz music.

I knew that our customers would enjoy the food, but I wanted to make the experience just as memorable. I wanted PizzaExpress to be addictive. I wanted diners to bound away from our restaurant straight to the pub.

I wanted them to tell the pub that PizzaExpress was the place to be. And then I wanted that whole pub to leave their pints and make a bee-line for our restaurants.

I felt that to polish off the PizzaExpress brand, we should introduce live music to the restaurants. This was a controversial idea – music in British eateries had forever been confined to the background. Something that you didn't really notice; something that diners probably wouldn't even be able to recall afterwards.

But I didn't care for the status quo. I wanted to put string quartets playing live in the middle of PizzaExpress restaurants. I felt the stereotype of 'a restaurant is to be seen and not heard' was outdated, and was sure that my customers would agree. It was a case of transporting the music of Ronnie Scott's into the dining room – a combination my two favourite things.

The string quartets would play once per week in our Wardour Street, Coptic Street and Fulham Road restaurants. For those unfortunate enough to never hear a string quartet, they are made up of two violinists, a violist and a cellist. And they make perfect music to complement a restaurant. The musicians changed every week, as did our waiting lists during the performances.

The customers couldn't get enough of it! And they came in their droves, every Wednesday evening, to eat food while the string quartet played. There was no additional price to the customer if they came on a string quartet night, even though there was of course an extra cost for me to hire them. I argued that the increased turnover made live music financially beneficial – much to the chagrin of the financial brain of my business partner, Ron.

He fastidiously studied the outgoings and showed that, although the restaurant was full to capacity, the cost of paying these skilled musicians actually meant that we were operating on a loss. But I didn't care much – I have never been driven by numbers. If I had the choice of giving a diner the best experience possible or making as much money as possible, there wouldn't even be a decision to be made. Plus, I always reasoned that a happy customer would become a returning customer.

Combined with the argument that our hard-working waitresses would get huge tips working those shifts, I managed to keep the financially demanding live music performances going.

We would take bookings long in advance for a table during a string quartet performance. With returning customers, I wanted to keep the quality of the acts high. It was relatively easy to create a buzz in Soho, but much more difficult to sustain one.

Inspired by this success, in 1969 I decided to turn the basement underneath the Wardour Street branch into the official PizzaExpress Jazz Club. The club soon became crammed with excited jazz lovers huddled around tables puffing on cigars to create that iconic, romantic, smoky atmosphere.

As buzz about the room spread through London, everybody seemingly agreed that there is no better pairing than jazz and pizza.

Tuesday nights were the big favourites – thanks largely to the incredibly talented PizzaExpress All Star Jazz Band who played that day of the week. The band boasted five remarkably talented musicians, who were put together by a musical genius I hired named Dave Bennett.

Dave was taken on to help with the running of the musical side of PizzaExpress. He could do it all – he was a top musician, agent, booker and producer.

His contact list was longer than a giraffe's necklace. He worked freelance for me, paid handsomely for each booking – and then of course there was the payment for the band as well. But Dave was immensely helpful, and we enjoyed a long and rich working relationship for decades.

He always had the best contacts to book up-and-coming musicians. At first it was local stars like Brian

Lemon and Lennie Felix, and over the years top names such as Sting, Jamie Cullum and Norah Jones would all go on to play in the PizzaExpress Jazz Club during their formative years. The Police were not really my cup of tea though, so please don't hold me responsible for giving Sting his break!

19
HOWZAT FOR A SPORTING FRIENDSHIP?

J azz also helped me form many strong friendships over the years, and none stronger than the camaraderie I have with cricket legend Doug Insole. Doug was vice-captain of the England national side, but I rarely watched cricket. My game was always hockey, and to a lesser extent football and tennis.

With my lack of cricketing knowledge, I must confess that I did not recognise this world-renowned sportsman when I first met him at a Henley Regatta in the late 1960s. He was the chairman of selectors and had wrapped up a career that included 450 first class cricket games just 10 years earlier. As you can imagine, Doug was used to being approached by strangers who knew his name.

However, while we both lined the banks of the Thames, there was only one thing that I recognised – his tie. He was sporting the distinctive maroon and gold tie with a golden hawk that could only mean one thing – this chap was a member of The Hawks' Club.

'The Hawks' is a members-only social club for sportsmen at the University of Cambridge. I had not been a member of the club, as my appearances for St Cat's at hockey, rugby and rowing never quite matriculated through to outings for the full university teams. But I had great respect for anyone blessed with the athletic ability to join the club.

I quickly went over and introduced myself, and Doug told me that he joined after representing the university at cricket and football. However, he never mentioned that he had gone on to represent England. He also kept under wraps that his football appearances led to a contract with Corinthian-Casuals, who he played for in the 1956 FA Amateur Cup final. Such was the modesty of a true member of the Hawks.

Similarly, during our first meeting, I did not mention that I had founded PizzaExpress. Business was going well and I was delighted that it was becoming a household name, but I didn't want to blow my own trumpet for the sake of it. Whilst I am a proud man, I am not a conceited one.

Although we got on like a house on fire, after we shook hands and went our separate ways after the regatta, I thought that I would likely never see this man again. It was very much a case of a bloke called Peter meeting a chap called Doug; it was not a matter of an upcoming entrepreneur meeting a cricket legend.

However, fate intervened and I gained a lifelong friend. Three days after the regatta, I had booked Kenny Baker to appear at the PizzaExpress Jazz Club. Kenny was a world-class trumpeter, comfortably the best in Britain, who had played with the likes of Frank Sinatra and Tony Bennett (as well as performing on numerous James Bond soundtracks).

As expected, the club was packed to the rafters for the performance – and one of the best things about owning the place was that I always got a well-positioned free seat. I came down the stairs to the club before the concert started and scanned the crowd. It was standing room only as they excitedly awaited Kenny's arrival. The crowd boasted the usual combination of beautiful women and well-to-do men, but there was one face that jumped out at me instantly.

It was Doug, the Cambridge Hawk from the regatta!

I went over and shook his hand, complemented him on being a fellow jazz fanatic and said how excited I was to have booked such a great musician. Doug was astounded – he had no idea that the stranger he briefly met three days previously ran this jazz club and pizza restaurant he regularly frequented.

I turned to his partner and jokingly asked if she thought Doug had kept any secrets from me, and she replied by saying, "Only if he didn't mention that he played cricket for England!" This was meant as a joke, but the bigger laugh came after I queried whether it was true.

After that, we exchanged numbers and have been firm friends ever since. The pair of us had both experienced a level of fame, although his far greater than mine, and I think the blissful naivety we shared for each other's professional lives helped us to create and consolidate our friendship.

While on the subject of socialising, I feel this is a good time to talk of my love of hockey. I have touched upon my love of the sport fleetingly, but it is such a large part of my life over such a long period of it that I would like to take a dalliance to discuss that wonderful game.

Ever since I first played as a boy at King's School in Peterborough, hockey was my sport of choice. I loved its fast pace, I loved the rough-and-tumble and I loved the skill involved in it. As a sport, it is similar to football – a ball game played on the ground where each side of eleven's sole ambition is to put the ball past a goal tender guarding a small frame.

Yet it has never got close to enjoying the same popularity that football ever did. That is because, although it is the greatest game in the world to play, it is not – nor will it ever be – a spectator sport.

The ball is too small and whizzes around the pitch too quickly to lend itself to being watched by large crowds. Ice hockey in America has prospered with large audiences, and I feel the reason for that is simply because the black puck is easy to follow against the white ice, whereas field hockey's smaller red ball can be lost on the green pitch.

After playing for teams in school and university, I fell out of competitive matches for many years, but was still known to pick up a stick and play from time-to-time. It was after coming back to London in the 1960s that I got back into the real swing of things after joining the Hampstead and Westminster Hockey Club.

The team's records dated back to 1890, when the Hampstead Cricket Club tried its hand at the sport. Four years later, the hockey club was formed. In the years since, Hampstead had dotted around London like a nomad looking for a permanent home, and when I arrived were playing games at the Hornsey Club in Crouch End – over five miles from Hampstead.

The fact that hockey failed to generate any money meant it was always a slog to keep the club running. We forever needed fund-raising efforts to improve the pitches or the club house. As my fortunes grew, I was delighted to be able to help out more in future years, and was graciously made Club President in later life.

We played in white shirts with vertical dark blue and light blue stripes, and boasted a truly fantastic side. We were never far off the top of the table, helped in no small way by our most talented player, Guy Mayers. Guy was a great friend off the pitch, and on it he would regularly win our silly post-match awards for 'most disruptive player' or 'most bewildering directional play'. At the back, goalkeeper Stan Elgar helped to keep our goals against column as low as possible.

Our league games were in London but we did travel to Bournemouth for hockey tournaments every Easter. As time drew on, I matriculated through to the Super Veterans LX Club, a team of players aged over 60, whom I went on to later represent in a match played in Holland.

Playing hockey, or any sport, gives a great sense of camaraderie. As Aristotle said, 'Man is a social animal', and a person clearly benefits from the close companionship. Team sports help one become more socially interactive – on the pitch and off it. The team spent a lot of time discussing new ideas, tactics and methods, bonded well and created a fantastic team spirit.

We also put on the most fantastic parties. Any excuse would do – Christmas, birthdays, anniversaries, births, post-match drinks – whenever we could get together, we would. Our parties were rather debaucherous, alcohol-fuelled affairs, though the presence of females (such as Stan's lovely wife Joyce) helped to keep them respectable.

Thanks to the work of our tireless secretary Norman Borrett, the club moved to the Paddington Recreation Ground in 1984. We were now even further (eight miles) from Hampstead, so the name 'Hampstead Hockey Club' was starting to look a little bit dated.

It was decided that we should rebrand as the 'Hampstead and Westminster Hockey Club', and I am very proud to still be their club president to this day.

Many years later to mark my 75th birthday, I organised for a jazz band to play in the train carriage that took them from London to Peterborough for the bash, and free champagne was served – what's the point of money if you can't treat your oldest friends?

At the party, the club presented me with a humorous statue of myself in full match day kit, which for years stood pride of place on a bookshelf in my living room before I donated it to the National Hockey Museum in Woking.

I can't speak highly enough of the sport of hockey, and the joy it has brought me in my life.

Another interesting socialising story came in 1971, when I was working in the Dean Street restaurant and a whole crowd was happily eating while being entertained by a jazz band. I scanned through the audience and spotted a familiar face – it was the singer and actor Bing Crosby, who was in town to play at The Palladium.

Of course, when one of the most famous men in the world is eating in your restaurant, you really have to go and say hello. I went over and introduced myself to the singer, and told him I was the man who was in charge of PizzaExpress. He was delighted by this news, and grabbed my hand to shake it. To my surprise, he excitedly told me that he had eaten in one of our branches the week before. He was a fellow pizza addict!

I invited Bing over to my flat opposite the restaurant, and there we put the world to rights over a few drinks. He was a very pleasant and modest man, not at all affected by the trappings of celebrity.

Bing told me that 'White Christmas' had sold 100 million copies around the world, but that it was not due to his performance. Instead, he claimed it simply showed the popularity of the festival of Christmas.

Such modesty both surprised and impressed me, as did his unforgettable quote that "a jackdaw with a cleft palate could have sung it successfully."

20
HEDGING MY BETS ON NEW INVESTMENTS

While PizzaExpress' stock rose faster than the Angel Gabriel with a severe case of homesickness, I was presented an exciting new opportunity to move into another business: The Connoisseur Casino.

Until then, my successes in business had been developing my own passion and vision, and I was a little worried of investing in other companies. The casino was a high-end members' club that was situated underneath our PizzaExpress in Fulham Road. Ted Box was the top man there, and I got to know him because of our close working proximity.

One afternoon, Ted came to speak to me with a proposition. He said the casino was always looking to expand, and asked whether I would like to be an investor. At first, I was a little unsure – I had never been a gambling man, and investing in such a business would go against the principle of working for what I enjoyed, rather than to make profits.

But Ted was a smooth talker. He took me into the casino, and I could see why it is addictive. The bright colours, the passionate customers and that fantastic, intangible feeling that fortunes are here to be won. In reality, they are there to be lost, and Ted explained to me that being an investor in a casino was a licence to print money. He said that "some of these people win a lot of money. But we *always* win more."

Ron, who I trusted implicitly on financial matters, went over the accounts and thought it would be a good deal. So I decided I should invest in it. I never put a huge amount of money into it, but enough for it to warrant a mention in this book.

I was a silent partner. I left Ted and a manager of Turkish descent (who I rarely met) to get on with the business. I would pop in as a customer from time-to-time, and as Ted predicted, I always lost more than I won. But there was something quite fun about losing money in a casino – your mood changes when you know that the person who will benefit from your poor fortune is yourself.

I stayed on as an investor until 1982, when I sold my shares after getting a generous offer from Trident TU. I thoroughly enjoyed my 12 years in the casino game, but it was always more of a folly than a venture that I truly fell in love with. I suppose I'm one of the few people to have enjoyed myself, made some money and then walked away from a casino, never to return.

But back in 1972, my salary from PizzaExpress was £80,000 per year. Of course, with all the combined assets

I was always valued higher than I actually was – which made bank visits in the search for a loan rather more easy than they are these days.

I was happy to promote the appearance of being a carefree millionaire, but I don't think I ever had anywhere near as much disposable income as people thought. I probably just lived so well that people thought I was richer than my bank balance suggested.

However, another expansion would last for even longer than those 12 years at the casino.

I decided that I wanted to create a venue that could host jazz music and sell pizzas simultaneously. It was a natural progression, after the success of the jazz nights in PizzaExpress. I started scouring London for a location for this restaurant, which I hoped would be the jewel in the business' crown.

I also had this idea that the new place should not be called 'PizzaExpress', to differentiate it from the existing restaurants. This was to be a jazz and cabaret venue that sold pizzas – not a pizzeria that sometimes hosted musicians.

We found a glorious spot on Hyde Park Corner, and as soon as I saw it the name came to me in a flash – "Pizza on the Park". It's a bit of a strange name, but the alliteration made it memorable, and highlighted two of the main selling points – our great pizza, and the salubrious surroundings of Hyde Park.

The company was set up under the newly formed company Peter Boizot (Franchises) Ltd, and was to be run separately from the PizzaExpress franchise. Although there were obvious similarities, this was a different business: one that focused more intently on music.

Perhaps the most important decision I made that paved the way for Pizza On The Park's success was putting my trusted employee Eddie Kidney in charge. He did a fabulous job, and under his stewardship the mixture of excellent, simple Italian cuisine and a consistently high standard of musical acts once again proved a hit.

Of course, as it was owned by me (and often run from the same Soho office that I used for PizzaExpress dealings), there was some confusion about the autonomy of the restaurant. Our meetings would often resemble the Mad Hatter's tea party; drinks and food were liberally passed around while we loudly debated ideas about each business, often changing which place we were talking about midway through the animated conversation – but it always made sense to me.

I put my stamp on the building, in my own usual way. Patrons would enter through a glass doorway with a semi-circular top, and then into the large airy restaurant (of course, with a signature 'open kitchen').

Potted palm trees splashed a dose of green between the tubular chairs, brown seats tucked under the white cloths of the many tables. Waiters dressed in black trousers and white aprons bustled around the customers, with trays laden with wine and warm refreshment.

There was also a basement, complete with its Steinway piano, and that is where the music took place.

I decided that, unlike the PizzaExpress Jazz Club, the live performances should not focus exclusively on one genre of music. It should be more eclectic. And so, I booked a diverse range of styles, from folk to funk, and from cabaret to classical.

The master of ceremonies of the music room was Simon Becker, a tall, grey-haired ex-officer in a smart cavalry regiment, who was also a pianist of extemporised jazz.

The first set would begin at around 9pm, and the room hushed. I would often come down and have a drink or two with whoever was performing. George Melly and the Footwarmers were personal favourites, but we would have all manner of household names perform on the stage. Cleo Lane, Johnny Dankworth, Marion Montgomery, Richard Rodney Bennett, Sheridan Morley – you name them, we booked them!

There were also famous people in the crowds, and American musician Larry Adler was there so often I renamed the room 'Larry's Room' – although that was as much testament to his musical ability as the frequency of his visits.

Friends joked that I must have done a deal with King Midas, as everything I touched seemed to be turning to gold. But I have always felt it was more a case of me enjoying the same things that lots of others did – music, pizza and partying. Why it took others so long to marry the three together as a business has always been a mystery to me.

However, the expansion into other businesses did not mean PizzaExpress' rise slowed down. Quite the opposite, in fact. An unexpected meeting would lead to me gaining a dear friend who would help us to push on the expansion of PizzaExpress more than I ever dreamed possible. The company received a phone call from a man named Moray Scot Dalgleish, an ex-cavalry officer who had been inspired after a visit to the PizzaExpress branch in Fulham Road.

At this point, there were six company-owned branches and all of them around London, and there was also the one franchise being run by Mario in Gloucester Road. Moray believed there was much greater scope for expansion, and he asked me if I had ever thought of opening a branch in Jersey.

The idea had never crossed my mind, but I was immediately receptive to it. My first thought was memories of a childhood holiday to the island just off the south coast of England. It had been my first ever overseas holiday, and this was my first chance of an overseas PizzaExpress expansion.

Moray told me that he was from Jersey, and although he was a regular visitor of London, he hoped to be able to run a PizzaExpress back on the island. I duly caught a ferry to Jersey, and the talk was immediately about where the restaurant would be, rather than how the logistics would work. I trusted Moray and was hell-bent on making his appealing vision of a Jersey branch come to life.

Within hours we had found a site. It was in Halkett Place, near to the market in St Helier. The nearby market meant footfall would never be a problem, and I was sure the good people of Jersey would love a pizza in preparation (or recovery from) a hard day's shopping.

Next, we had to talk business. When you are dealing with a gentleman like Moray, business is easy to do. There was no haggling over prices – we both just wanted something reasonable to get the ball rolling. We agreed on a 50/50 split of the profits, and that deal stood for the next 23 years without a single problem.

I helped Moray getting the business off the ground, but it was very much him who was in charge of the franchise.

He hired a splendid Italian man named Rino Bertozzi to help with the day-to-day management of the restaurant, and was ready to open for business in late August 1971.

Sadly, it was not an immediate success. In the first week, the branch took just over £100 – considerably less than any of the London equivalents (and lower than the weekly running costs). I got a phone call from a rather exasperated Moray, who told me of his disappointment at the initial takings. I laughed, and told him that maybe those market shoppers needed a little bit of time to get used to the pizzeria.

I have never lacked confidence in any of my restaurants, or any venture that I have ever run. Some may mistake my confidence for pig-headed arrogance, but more often than not things turned out for the best in the end.

Thankfully, that is what happened with the Jersey branch. Within a few weeks, business started to pick up and, within a few years, it was regularly matching the takings from the best supporting London restaurants.

Ron and I were so impressed with how Moray had created this well-run franchise overseas that we asked if he would become PizzaExpress' official 'Franchise Controller'. This neologism related to a new role to seek out new franchises and set them up with PizzaExpress restaurants. Moray gladly accepted the opportunity, and was placed into the rare position of being both an employee as well as a fellow director.

The company already had an extremely successful core of restaurants. They offered fantastic value for money. Despite the fact we were adding franchises, I was very hands-on in every restaurant – coaching pizzaiolos, inspecting the loos, encouraging the staff. If I was in a restaurant and saw a pizzaiolo stretching dough with a rolling pin, instead of by hand, I would immediately dash into the kitchen and give them a piece of my mind.

The franchise model gave people like Moray and Mario a lot of autonomy, but there was no doubt that they were divisions of my parent group of 'PizzaExpress'. Not least, I ensured that each restaurant stuck to the iconic interior designs of the PizzaExpress restaurants, as shown by this sketch of what I wanted the new franchise in Richmond, Surrey, to look like.

Obviously, the counter was primarily a barrier cutting off the 'dining' and 'cooking' areas. But it was a lot more than that. It snaked around the restaurant in a cursive pattern, creating a modern, almost pop-art design.

To help me keep high standards throughout the organisation, I would often send a loyal employee named Lewis Winstock to inspect the branches. He was a tall, lanky Oxford graduate who, like me, was married to PizzaExpress. He devoted his days and nights to PizzaExpress.

In his (seemingly rare) moments of leisure, the workaholic Lewis occupied himself with military music and wrote a book called *Songs and Music of the Redcoats*. He died, tragically, of cancer as a young man in 1977, but he was an integral cog in the rapid expansion of PizzaExpress.

21
PROTECTING
PRICELESS SOHO

Despite all this external expansion, Soho still had my heart. It was during one of my regular drinking sessions in The Colony Room, which was run by the extraordinary Muriel Belcher, that I was introduced to a social movement that was gathering steam to protect the borough from a most deplorable threat.

There were serious concerns for the future of the area I had grown to call my second home. Peterborough was still a base, especially with my mother living there, but Soho had provided me with everything I had asked for since moving there in 1965. But by 1972, there were concerns that what made it great may be about to be lost.

Developers were circling around Soho, and neighbouring Piccadilly. The area was the beating heart of London, and rumours were rife that developers wanted to exploit its value to the maximum by turning its charming buildings into high-rental flats. What a travesty – this was the area that had housed and inspired some of the world's greatest thinkers, such as Karl Marx, Isaac Newton and William Blake.

The government was unlikely to intervene – why would they want to stop this attempt to kick-start the struggling economy? In January of that year, unemployment had topped 1 million for the first time since the 1930s – it had been just 580,000 when Ted Heath's Conservative government came to power less than two years before. The Tories were cutting services and relying on private investment to get the economy out of the doldrums. One couldn't see them spurning the opportunity to turn swinging Soho into a lucrative housing market.

With Soho earmarked for destruction, action needed to be taken in 1972. And so, along with some like-minded people, I went along to a meeting room at Kettner's restaurant, in Romilly Street. Thelma Seear had hired it out and invited residents and traders along to discuss what was happening.

The room was big enough to seat 30 people, but 150 turned out in force to discuss what was happening to the borough. It was during that meeting that the Soho Society was born.

Our purpose was to be a lobby group to the Greater London Council, but also in our sights was the Ministry of the Environment, who we pinpointed a key figure in helping to retain the area's charms. We vowed to hold monthly meetings to raise awareness of concerning applications that had been submitted... clearly with the intention of planning how to sabotage them and protect our beloved area.

I was made secretary, while Leslie Hardcastle was named the chairman. Leslie was a film man, who worked his way up through the British Film Institute and the National Film Theatre, and valued Soho so highly that he would often film in the area. But the beating heart of the Soho Society was Ed Berman, an American of unusually charming persuasion who dedicated himself to frustrating the re-development proposals which would have destroyed the borough I loved.

Our official mantra was purposefully vague, *"To make Soho a better place in which to live, work or visit."* We were there to protect the borough, but also to protect its businessmen. There should be more things like that.

There certainly ought to be something like the Soho Society around on the High Streets up and down England today, where new businesses seem to open and close within 12 months. Not enough advice is available to entrepreneurs, and without their success our economy will never grow.

We were always lobbying MPs and councillors. We were trying to help people in the running of their businesses and restaurants. There was no payment, nor an implication that we would want our favours to be returned. We genuinely just wanted to see other businesses, and this magnificent borough, to continue to thrive.

Soho has got an unfortunate reputation for being a little bit seedy. I never agreed with that – I thought it was just incredibly diverse. Yes, there were brothels and sex shops, not to mention a large gay scene. But it also had immense heritage, dating back to the 17th century influx of French Huguenots.

We wanted to retain Soho as a place for drunken writers, poets and artists to remain crammed into pubs and restaurants – without that, they may have sobered up long enough to become bores!

We were worried that outside intervention would see the rates go through the roof, driving out the smaller businessman. We held the tide back for as long as we could, but regrettably that is what has now happened. Soho is now a rather limp parody of what it once was, and it's all because the cost of rates and rent has priced the true artisans out of the market.

But in the 1970s and 1980s, we were a strong pressure group. We had a presence at every Westminster City Council meeting and would relentlessly campaign for the otherwise forgotten common man.

Of course, we also had lots of parties. You would bring 'friends' to meet 'pals' who were enjoying drinks with 'chums', and of course strangers there were always hoping to make new acquaintances. We had good quality wine and champagne. We gorged on a variety of cuisines. We would go out together almost every night of the week. It was tremendous.

I must say, our pressure group was warmly welcomed by Westminster City Council – maybe they thought we would help alleviate some of the work off them. Within months of forming, the city council gave us formal consultative status for all planning, environmental, traffic and even licensing matters (although when we discussed the latter there were more than a few 'declarations of interest' to be made, as you can imagine).

Once we had that, we were less of a lobby group… and more a wing of the local authority. With this newly-found influence, we were able to persuade Westminster City Council to make Soho into a conservation area – thus eradicating our fears of the impending demolitions.

22
EXPRESSING THE NEED
FOR AN EXECUTIVE TEAM

Towards the end of the 1970s, the PizzaExpress dynamic changed to include an executive team that helped to mould the way the company was run.

In 1978, I appointed a dynamic young man from Yorkshire named Ian Neill to help with our franchising operations. Ian was a bright spark with a strong business brain, which would eventually bring Japanese food to the British High Street after he steered Wagamama's dynamic rise from having two restaurants in 1998 to branches all over the world within a decade.

I would like to think that the successes he had there were, in some part, related to his time at PizzaExpress. Ian has kindly referred to me as a mentor of sorts, and that is something I feel very proud about. I am also proud of the fact that I can see traces of the PizzaExpress story in his successes at Wagamama.

Another person who came into the fold as a director was David Page, who like Eddie Kidney had worked his way from a part-time pot washer. He started with us while training to become a teacher, but soon moved up the catering ladder due to being a good worker and extremely dedicated to the company.

David took out a second mortgage and a loan of £6,000 to buy a PizzaExpress franchise in Chiswick. He made a success of it, inevitably, and would end up buying a total of 14 PizzeExpress franchises under the name G&F Fundings.

Like Ian, he went on to create another high-street chain – the incredibly successful Gourmet Burger Kitchen. As with Wagamama, I like to think it is a restaurant that has PizzaExpress coursing through its DNA.

I am happy for his successes, but I never knew David particularly well on a personal basis. There was no animosity; we were just not cut from the same cloth. I was a food lover driven by a desire to create dining experiences. David was a businessman: a man who dealt with numbers, not subjective matters such as how much the customers enjoyed the dining experience.

I say this with the hope that it does not insult David. There is nothing wrong with a businessman being driven by profit margins. To be honest, that is probably the reason why David is still in *The Times'* Rich Lists and I am not.

The other people in my inner circle have already been mentioned – Moray Scot Dalgleish, Eddie Kidney and of course Ron Simson. All of my directors went on to be very successful (and very rich) men, and I take great pride in helping them to get on in life.

With a core of strong employees in place, I was a little less hands-on with PizzaExpress and could afford to look at other ambitions. After all of the lobbying of Whitehall and Westminster, I was well and truly gripped by the political bug. Back in Peterborough I had been a well-known supporter of the Liberal Party, not to be confused with the Liberal Democrats, for a number of years.

The party had a youthful zip in Peterborough, and as a 45-year-old still with a teenager's outlook on like, its policies of social liberalism were very similar to my own.

The Liberal Party had rather died off after World War Two, but in the '70s was experiencing something of a renaissance under the leadership of Jeremy Thorpe. Free trade, minimal government intervention and personal liberty were their key concepts, and I was a committed party member. The party did well in local elections, but had routinely struggled to get seats in Parliament.

In the 1950s and 1960s, the Liberal candidates got less votes than my ugly mug would generate in a beauty contest. But then at the start of the 1970s, a revival had seen Liberal candidates jump up to having around 15 percent of the national vote.

With the swing in an upward trajectory, I was approached by the Peterborough Liberal Party with an intriguing proposal: to stand for election to become the MP for Peterborough for the election in February, 1974. The incumbent politician was the Conservative Harmar Nicholls, and had been since 1950. He was a building-construction manager by background. In power for 24 years, Harmar had been a high-flying governmental minister under Anthony Eden and Harold Macmillan from 1955 until 1961, but after that his popularity started to wane.

The Liberal Party felt that, with a bit of the old Boizot charm, they might be able to take a high-profile seat from the all-powerful Conservative party. The basis for targeting Harmar stemmed from him being subject to one of the most marginal electoral victories one could imagine. In the 1966 general election, he clung on to his seat by just three votes (23,944 votes to Labour's 23,941).

It's amazing to think that if one extra family in Peterborough had turned out to vote, the whole city would have had a different MP.

He held on to his seat again in the 1970 election, but the writing seemed on the wall by 1974. Sadly, the Liberal Party was always a distant third, so I knew that it would be an uphill struggle if I was to stand for election.

But I wouldn't be Peter Boizot if I only stood because I thought I would win. I thought it would be good fun and a magnificent experience just to contest the election – to be victorious would be the icing on the cake. So I agreed to represent the Liberal Party in the election.

It would take all of my efforts to concentrate on the canvassing, and so I took a month off from PizzaExpress. As much as I didn't think it was likely I would win the election, I respected the democratic process too much to not put my all into the battle. I put Ron in charge of the day-to-day operations while I focused on the election campaign.

I trusted Ron implicitly with the business – he had been there almost from the start, after all. I gave him my word that I would return to the top chair whether the election bid was successful or not (although I did not have a clue how the logistics of that professional duality would work).

I suppose I would have just not slept!

CHAPTER V:
THE NECKLACE TURNS INTO AN EMPIRE

Step five in making a pizza is patience. You must wait for the oven to do its job – there is little to do but wait for it to be cooked. Although you should monitor it to make sure the pizza is not cooking incorrectly, if all is going according to plan you shouldn't fiddle unnecessarily.

Similarly, a successful business should not be fiddled with unnecessarily. If it is popular, don't change the formula. And so, by the late 1970s I was able to delegate much of the day-to-day running of PizzaExpress to my highly competent executives, allowing me to focus on new ambitions.

23
CAN PIZZA LEAD TO PARLIAMENT?

LIBERAL

PETER BOIZOT
FROM PETERBOROUGH
FOR PETERBOROUGH

Published by Paul Froggitt, Election Agent, 5 Mary Armyne Road, Peterborough; and Printed by G. H. Fisher and Sons (Printers) Ltd., 209 Dogsthorpe Road, Peterborough

The first thing I did after taking that impromptu semi-sabbatical was pick up a telephone and call the news desk at the *Peterborough Evening Telegraph*, the city's daily newspaper. They had a good circulation, and I knew that getting your mug in the paper was the most immediate way of getting people's attention. I organised to meet up with a reporter and the story that 'Mr PizzaExpress was running for election in Peterborough' became front page news the next day. What a way to make an impact.

They wrote a very fair piece on me, saying I was coming in with the enthusiasm of a badger in mating season, but with a modest political background.

A lot of people give the press a bad name, but I have always found local newspapers to be incredibly balanced and unbiased… I suppose the difference is their reporters live in the community they write about. If somebody writes a bad piece about you and you see them in the pub, you are going to let them know their inaccuracies.

But the nationals are a little more distant from their readership, which means they don't mind embellishing facts to the point of fabrication.

The day after the story hit the shops, I took a walk through Cathedral Square, in the centre of Peterborough, and I had never felt so famous – but was being afforded a different kind of recognition. People approached me to congratulate me on being selected to stand, and then in the next breath rattling off a long list of problems they were encountering (and often unrealistically expected the next MP to solve).

Everything from late buses to a lack of primary school places – all of the ills and ailments that a city's people can have. This gave me a (somewhat terrifying) glimpse into what life as an MP must be like. It also explained why politicians with brown hair see it quickly turn white (and why politicians with grey hair quickly go bald).

I knew it would be a stretch to win the election – the majority of the electorate vote as they did when they were 18 years old, and third-party candidates had struggled to get any traction in Peterborough before. But I wanted to make an impact, whether it was to put the cat among the pigeons or pull off an unlikely electoral victory for the Liberals.

I worked closely during the election campaign with a splendid chap named David Powell, a fellow Liberal 10 years my senior who ran Sacrewell Farm, in Thornhaugh (just north of Peterborough). David helped me to knock on thousands of doors all over the city. We had an electorate of 62,507, and I'll be damned if we didn't talk to every last one of them.

This was a return to my days selling Compton's Encyclopaedia. The old salesmen tricks came back into play. I got my hands on the electoral role, and before knocking on any door I would know the person who lived in the house's name.

Such small tricks make an instant impression that you are not a nuisance knocking indiscriminately on doors, but that you are there to speak to that resident specifically. By sharing names, they are less likely to ignore you.

And after I had let Mr and Mrs X know that I was Mr B, I gave them a passionate spiel not about why they should vote for me – but why they should vote for my policies.

If a man answered, I would discuss how giving the worker power will get us out of the country's financial problems. If a woman answered, I would talk about how a switch to free market economics would help their children find a job in 10 years' time. A little sexist by today's standards, but those were the things I felt men and women were interested in back in the 1970s.

For the most part, people were interested in what I had to say. I do remember one stuffy Conservative in Longthorpe (the rich west end of Peterborough) scoffing at the principle of a Liberal MP presiding over his constituency and slamming the door in my face… along with some stern instructions to get off his lawn.

When people weren't in, we would put a glossy A4 pamphlet through their door. On the front was a magnificently striking headshot of myself, framed with a bright orange rim (the colour of the Liberals) and the slogan 'Peter Boizot: From Peterborough For Peterborough'. On the back was a list of my policies, which were more important than my name.

Much like with restaurants – a good politician needs no bush… but a little bit of razzamatazz helps make a good first impression and get their attention. But without good policies, you would never win a vote in a Parliamentary election. That is why in Britain, we don't get actors and celebrities becoming politicians.

The election fell on Thursday, February 28, 1974. I was tired but excited when I woke up at 5am to liaise with David, who had offered to drive me to every single polling station for some last minute campaigning. We weren't as slick as the Conservatives or Labour, who had pinpointed marginal areas for their campaign – we just wanted to go into every area and appeal personally for every possible vote.

And that's exactly what we did – we picked off the city ward-by-ward at each of the 19 polling stations. However, one eluded us – the rural, well-to-do village of Upton. It was a tiny polling station, and almost certainly everyone there would vote Conservative, but we spent more time looking for that church hall there than on any of the other wards. It was rather farcical, driving around in his battered old farming van looking for this tiny polling station where anything less than a 90 percent Conservative turnout would be a shock.

But the 1966 result kept playing on my mind… three votes, just three votes. That could be the difference between me being plain old Peter Boizot or Peter Boizot, MP for Peterborough. But David and I never did find that battered old polling station, and had to give up on the ward to continue our last-minute campaigning.

When it got to 10pm and the polling stations were closed, we jumped back into the van and hot-footed it to the Town Hall – usually the home of Peterborough City Council, but on this night dedicated to counting votes to decide who would represent the city in Parliament, and maybe even who would represent the country in government.

As a venue, the Town Hall symbolised all that was so magnificent about Britain, but it also summed up the cause of many problems she faced. The grandiose building had housed the local authority since 1933, with splendid ceremonial rooms such as the Mayor's Parlour and Council Chamber. It was a truly wonderful setting, but there was a part of me that wondered whether the politicos should be enjoying its splendour while the rest of the country scrapes by during those difficult times.

The counters sat in the magnificent Mayor's Parlour, where portraits of previous first citizens of Peterborough sat on a golden wall. The ballots were emptied on one table, given to somebody to unravel and then given to another person to put them into piles for each candidate.

It was invitation-only inside the Mayor's Parlour, very much only for election officials and candidates. I had polite conversations with Conservative candidate Mr. Nicholls, who didn't express much emotion despite predictions of a tight race, and Labour candidate Michael Ward, who was a bag of nerves. I was rather enjoying the whole experience.

The mounds of paper looked disproportionately large on the Labour and Conservative side, as could be expected. But mine still maintained about a fifth of the votes, which I felt was a good result for my first time in an election against two seasoned pros. With Mr Ward and Mr Nicholls standing eagle-eyed over the counters, I felt a bit more laid-back about the whole thing.

I decided to take a break from the stuffy parlour and walk out and see what was happening in the rest of Town Hall. There was a cacophony of noise as people lined the stairwell and halls of the marble-floored building. The Labour supporters milled on ground level, while the Tories were on the upper floor, all proudly wearing their rosettes as if they were supporting their football team at a Wembley FA Cup final.

I had a nice conversation with Peterborough City Council Cllr Charles Swift – who represented the same area of town I grew up in. Cllr Swift reminded me that we were the same age and he had already served 20 years of public service, but never been a Parliamentary candidate – yet here I was, waltzing in fresh off the street into an election!

I am sure Charles was joking. He has never struck me as having any political ambitions other than to diligently serve as a councillor for the city of Peterborough (and specifically the area of New England). His mother Maud Swift had been the fourth female Mayor of Peterborough in 1959, and the Swifts were held in great regard around the city. Indeed, Charles still is – he still serves his city council ward diligently, and you can see him cycling to constituents' houses despite being 84 years old. That is the way I would have liked to be as an MP.

At around 1.20am, the call was made that the count had been made and verified, and all candidates must gather at the top of the marble staircase for the revelation over who won. The previously unflappable Conservative candidate finally showed some emotion, looking visibly distressed that he may have finally lost his seat.

The Mayor, Cllr Raymond Laxton, said that 51,456 votes had been cast. The figures were read out like three barrels of a gun being fired off;

"Boizot, Peter, of the Liberal party: 10,772 votes.

"Nicholls, Harmar, of the Conservative party: 20,353.

"Ward, Michael, of the Labour party: 20,331."

I was delighted; over 20 percent of the vote was given to me – almost treble the support the previous Liberal candidate received. The bigger story was that Harmar had held onto his seat by the skin of his teeth – he was just 22 votes away from being ousted. It wasn't quite a family that decided the election this time, but certainly one street could have made all the difference.

I congratulated Harmar, and commiserated with Michael. Both were good, honourable men and it was no stain on my character to have been defeated by either. Many well-wishers came my way and congratulated me on a good first electoral showing, and most urged me to come back for the next election in four or five years.

Such plaudits certainly whetted my appetite for a second bite at the cherry.

24
POLITICAL ELECTIONS ARE LIKE LONDON BUSES

However, one prominent Labour city councillor left a sour taste in my mouth. He pulled me into one of Town Hall's many nooks and privately lambasted me for "stealing votes" from the Labour candidate.

One could see his logic – 30,000 people had voted for left-wing Liberal and Labour candidates, yet it was the 20,000 who voted for the right-wing Tory who won the election. If my 10,772 votes were to be divvied up, it's likely that more would have fallen to the left-wing Labour candidate than the right-wing Conservative. Certainly more than enough to fulfil that 22 vote swing.

The councillor, who undoubtedly had ambitions of cuddling up with a Labour MP for Peterborough, was incredulous at the fact I had stood between him and his schemes for power. He said that by standing, I had distorted democracy. "Ruined the vote", he squealed – dismissing me as a niche celebrity candidate who had distorted the election.

I won't reveal his name in this book, out of respect to his family members. But let's just say he was an odious type who reminded me of the worst type of customers in PizzaExpress, who would often stay long after the bill had been served debating who should pay it than being pleasant and evenly splitting the bill like gentlemen.

His assertion that I had distorted the vote left me with three overwhelming emotions. I felt at once enraged, disappointed and invigorated by his opinion.

If the public thought of me as a paper candidate, I wouldn't have tallied over 10,000 votes. What kind of a 'democracy' only allows people to run for election if they are going to win? The councillor held the public in such little regard that he dismissed Mr Nicholls' fair election victory as a fluke. The plurality of people chose Mr Nicholls over Mr Ward, and regardless of the margin of the victory, a fair win is a fair win.

His attitude made me determined to stand once again for an election. In politics like in business, I have always been a cantankerous soul. This criticism was like throwing a red rag at a bull. If my appetite to run again had been whetted by the plaudits, it was well and truly drenched by the councillor's vile opinions. I told him that not only do I reject his opinion, but that it would inspire me for the next electoral campaign. However, one thing that did come as a surprise was just how soon that next vote would occur.

It was not just the election in Peterborough that had been close – the pattern was replicated all over the country. The election in February 1974 was the first since the Second World War that didn't see one party win the majority of the votes.

Of Parliament's 630 seats, 301 were won by Labour and 297 by the Conservatives. The other 32 were a spattering of Liberals (14), and various smaller parties. My beloved Liberals had performed well all over the country, and at the same time I was getting collared by that Labour councillor, the real Labour politicians were preparing to set up a coalition with the successful Liberals.

Eventually, it became obvious that rather than trying to cobble together a government through cross-party deals, a second election should be called in October. And so, after 45 years of never contesting an election, I had my opportunity to stand for the second time in eight months. My opponents would be the same two people – Harmar Nicholls and Michael Ward. To use a football analogy, it was time to dust off those rosettes for an FA Cup Final replay.

This time, I took just two weeks off work before the election, in the hope that the voters would remember me and my policies. Again, I put poor old Ron in charge of the business. David no doubt left his wife in charge of Sacrewell Farm. We again started knocking on doors, and you could feel that the public were not as engaged for this election. Apathy is the wrong word, but there was certainly a feeling of "oh, not this again". There is a reason elections usually come around every five years rather than every eight months.

On the day of the vote, David and I pulled the same trick of visiting every polling station, but despite hitting all the hot spots, I finished the campaign feeling a bit flat. As we pulled into Town Hall for the count, I said to my trusted driver David that I feared my support had dwindled, perhaps even halved.

Faster than in February, the votes had been collated and the result was in. The feeling was that Labour would finally knock Harmar from his seat this time around, and I had a feeling that my Liberal supporters may defect to tactically vote Labour in a bid to remove him from power.

New Mayor Jack Farrell announced the result of the election;

"Boizot, Peter, of the Liberal Party: 7,302 votes.

"Nicholls, Harmar, of the Conservative Party: 19,972.

"Ward, Michael, of the Labour Party: 21,820."

I felt some sympathy for Harmar – a man who had served Peterborough so well for 24 years. The dejection on his face combined with the insensitive sneers of the supporters of the victorious opposition left a sour taste in my mouth.

Partisan schadenfreude: is that really what I wanted to subject myself to? Maybe it was because I'd just lost again, with fewer votes than I had managed to get previously, but I started to wonder whether political life was for me.

I never ran for election again, but I have remained involved in the political sphere. I am the president of the Peterborough Liberal Democrats (despite being a Liberal, rather than a Liberal Democrat), and meet regularly with both Liberal Democrat and Liberal councillors in Peterborough. I am also proud to count the Liberal Democrats' national leader Nick Clegg as a fan of mine.

I met Nick, who is now the deputy Prime Minister, at a Lib Dem function in London back in 2008. We had a very cordial, brief chat, where I explained my political ties to the Liberal cause, and he politely listened and I thought that was that. But, less than a minute after he had left, Nick rushed back and again shook my hand. "I've just been told you created PizzaExpress. You never told me – I love that place!", he excitedly said.

I have sympathy for the Lib Dems who now find themselves in a hung Parliament, aligned with the Conservatives. People like to criticise them for dropping policies in their manifesto after getting into bed with the Tories, but one must remember that Nick Clegg made that manifesto imagining being in power – not imagining sharing power. The money saved by axing Trident would have meant tuition fees were never introduced.

25
VENICE IS IN PERIL

A nyway, back to the mid-1970s – Harold Wilson was the new Prime Minister and I had been kicked into the political gutter by an uninterested electorate.

This was also the period that I grew what was to become my trademark moustache. I have always felt they add a touch of distinction to a gentleman's upper lip. A beard, or worse still stubble, looks unkempt. But treated well, like my thick lip-warmer was, they can look smart yet quirky. I felt it complimented my eccentric personality. I would sport this moustache for many years to come, and its spurting coincided with yet another spurt of interest in another project.

With my ties to Italy ever-strengthening as PizzaExpress grew, I had begun to look upon the country less as a holiday or business destination and more as a family member. And during the 1970s, she was unwell. It was a depressing decade for the country.

It started with Italy being thrashed 4-1 in the football World Cup Final by Brazil, a defeat that hit me as hard as an England loss. Then things became much more serious. There was much social unrest, with workers' strikes and feminist protests, as well as horrific terrorist activities and even a neo-fascist revival – a far cry from the country that had embraced me so warmly in 1948.

However, such problems can be rectified with social change. Once there were jobs and money, the aforementioned problems would reduce rapidly. The real concern for me was a very urgent threat that could ruin a whole city, and a beautiful one at that.

On November 4 and 5 of 1966, there had been great floods in Florence and Venice. The disaster led to donations pouring in from all over the world, especially for Venice. The floods showed just how precarious this magnificent city in northeast Italy was – and how close its 118 islands were to being submerged under a bed of sea.

'The Floating City' looked in danger of becoming 'The Flooded City'.

Venice is unlike any other city on Earth. It is connected by more than 400 bridges, most over beautiful canals with gondolas coasting along. It is the world's most tranquil city – largely because it is the world's only non-motorised city. Despite being a lover of such vehicles, I feel that the absence of cars, buses and motorbikes gives it the most wonderful ambience.

Replacing those conventional modern modes of transport were far more elegant, traditional types – gondolas floating along the rivers, transporting people between the beautiful buildings of Venice. However, those amazing waterways were now threatening to destroy the city.

Venice had always been threatened by flood tides coming from the Adriatic. The problems started every autumn and ended every spring, meaning the city was only safe during the summer. Venetian politicians had levied a stamp tax to pay for flood relief, but with only approximately 250,000 people living in Venice, they had no chance of raising enough money. The city was sinking, and its lovely old buildings were in great danger of being lost. If something wasn't done soon, it could become the new 'lost city of Atlantis'.

Little to my knowledge, a small charity had been set up in England to counter the problems. The 'Venice in Peril Fund' had been running since the great Italian floods of 1966. Initially known as the Art and Archives Rescue Fund in 1967, it had been streamlined to exclusively help Venice in 1971.

A friend told me that they fund-raised throughout the year to help restore Venetian monuments, buildings and works of art, and to keep them safe from the impending doom that further floods would bring. I thought it was fantastic that a band of people from England would create a charity to raise money for something so far afield. They say charity begins at home, but in this case it came from thousands of miles away.

It was also somewhat fitting that it would be Lord Norwich who spearheaded the group. Not only is the Anglian coast one of the hot-spots for flooding in Britain, but tucked away in the East of England, Norwich is one of the closest cities to my hometown of Peterborough.

I couldn't stop thinking of this band of philanthropists from East Anglia who were so admirably trying to save something that didn't impact on their everyday lives. While everyone else was worrying about losing cash through taxes and how their pensions were shaping up, these fantastic people were concerned about giving money to stop a city in a foreign country flooding.

The idea came to me that if we only took a small donation from every customer, we could help to save this fantastic city. Of course, there were two stumbling blocks to these ambitions – would the customers pay extra, and what would the other executives involved in the business think? I wanted to help Venice, but I didn't want to bankrupt PizzaExpress while doing it.

In private, I consulted with Ron about what we could do. I didn't want anyone else know about my desire to partner up with Venice In Peril, because it would get the charity's hopes up if it turned out to be impossible.

Ron was unsure about the idea – he couldn't understand why an English business would be helping *Venice*. He quite rightly pointed out that there were hundreds of extremely worthy causes that need money in Britain – and dozens in Peterborough or London. Why, he wondered, was I so interested in saving Venice?

There is no logical answer to that question. All I could say was that I felt that the loss of Venice would be a great loss to future generations. I imagined a future where people were bereft of the chance of seeing this most wonderful city.

I suppose it also stems from the fact that my success with PizzaExpress was so heavily reliant on Italy and her culture. What's the use in selling Italian food if Italian culture is being lost underwater? Maybe this was my way of paying back to the culture that I had borrowed from to create my successful business.

I passionately explained the quandary to my business partner Ron, and he knew that in reality this was not a discussion – it was me telling him the new venture PizzaExpress was about to embark upon. The only thing to discuss was how we would get our customers' money into the Venice In Peril coffers.

Ron was firm in his opinion that our customers would not take kindly to any sort of increase in prices to go towards this cost – thinking it as a 'stealth tax' to be imposed on British pizza eaters to preserve Italian heritage.

I argued that our customers were liberal, progressive thinkers who wouldn't think so cynically about contributing a small fund towards a worthy cause – it's not like the price was increased just to thicken Peter Boizot's wallet.

Yet I respected Ron's business sense, harking back to those wise pointers that helped PizzaExpress get off the ground in the first place. A compromise was needed, and in the end, it was obvious.

We decided to keep prices the same, but politely asked for a voluntary donation towards the cause. I thought that five pence per pizza would be affordable for our diners, and by making it discretionary removed Ron's rather ominous prediction that our customers would think of it as a stealth tax.

26
THE PIZZA VENEZIANA

I thought it would be best for the Venice In Peril Fund donations to come from a specific pizza, created specifically for this fund-raiser. This would again distance the dish from Ron's ominous 'stealth tax' fears. And so, the Pizza Veneziana was born.

With so much of me personally invested in the initiative, it was to be a vegetarian option of course. Some thought it was a shame to not eat fish, because that was such a traditionally Venetian ingredient, but there is plenty of other food from that wonderful city to choose from – and that is exactly what I did.

The ingredients included a savoury marinade that had been popular in Venice since the Middle Ages – rich with red onions, capers, olives, pine kernels and sultanas. The pizza would cost 90 pence to order – with a discretionary charge of five pence to go towards the Fund. To put that into context, a glass of house wine in those days was 45 pence – so the dish was cheap, and the discretionary charge more than affordable.

I hoped that our diners would put more than five pence into the pot, and that the donations from our thousands of customers would make a real financial impact, as well as raising awareness.

After getting everything in motion, I made a trip to speak to the chairman and trustees at Venice In Peril. Despite having Lord Norwich as their figurehead, the organisation was rather inevitably based in London.

I explained to Lord Norwich that I was a great lover of the heritage of Venice. He then proceeded to blow me out of the water with both his knowledge and prior activism. He explained that he was an honorary chairman of the World Monuments Fund and a vice-president of the National Association of Decorative and Fine Arts Societies.

He was also a lover of British heritage and a vocal member of the National Trust – where he would go on to serve for many years as a member of the Executive Committee. This was a man who knew what he was doing – a man I knew I could trust.

Lord Norwich was delighted to hear of my intentions to use PizzaExpress to help their worthy cause. He introduced me to the founders of the Fund's committee – Sir Ashley Clarke, who had been ambassador in Rome from 1952 to 1962, a delightful woman called Natalie Brook and, most memorably, Carla Thorneycroft.

Carla, who I should probably call 'Lady Thorneycroft', was the wife of former Chancellor of the Exchequer Lord Peter Thorneycroft, was another of the trustees. She had grown up in Venice, but moved to England in her teens. Carla was an effortlessly beautiful woman, who had been employed by Vogue as a fashion editor. Even before getting involved with Venice in Peril, she had worked diligently to help Florence – and was appointed a member of the Italian Order of Merit in 1967.

Carla was the wrong side of 60 years old in 1974, but still undoubtedly a beautiful woman – both inside and out.

We got some welcome publicity about the new pizza – a few of the national newspapers picked up on the idea. I also cajoled some photographers to come down for the official launch of the Pizza Veneziana, and my ugly mug got into the reviews.

As it turned out, the pizza was very successful – in terms of sales, in terms of funds raised, and (perhaps most importantly) in terms of raising awareness for the very real concerns that Venice was facing. On the menu, a discretionary asterisk was placed next to the Pizza Veneziana that told the customer about how making a donation would help the long-term defence of the city – both as a monument and a living community.

Immediately, the initiative struck a chord with the customers. They came in their swarms to take in this new pizza that could save a sinking city – and I never heard a case of somebody deciding against paying the five pence discretionary fund. In fact, people seemed to believe that figure was too low – and most began to offer more than the asked for amount.

It was obvious that we were onto a winner, and that the five pence fee was too low. So we increased the advised donation to 25 pence – again, purely at the discretion of the customer. I raised it to this (still modest) amount because I felt the donations we had already received would help Venice over the next five years.

But I wanted to help them for the next 25 years. To hell with that, I wanted to help Venice for the next 500 years – to protect it for future generations.

The newly raised suggested fee was matched ably by our customers. I still think that Ron was probably right to make it a discretionary fee, but the fear that our customers in England would not care about hardships in Italy thankfully proved to be unfounded.

I am very proud that, to this day, the Pizza Veneziana remains on the PizzaExpress menu, and the restaurant remains a major benefactor for the Venice In Peril fund.

The two entities have worked together to get extensive national media coverage and put on numerous other fund-raisers. Those at Venice In Peril tell me that it is probably the longest relationship between a business and a charity in the UK. The charity is still run by a small committed team of people, and I maintain an active role and still sit in on board meetings. The directors are very appreciative towards PizzaExpress' help, and I hope the relationship continues long after I leave this mortal coil.

In 2011, the amount raised by the Pizza Veneziana for the cause tipped over a whopping £2 million. I didn't ever dream that it would raise so much money, and I hadn't thought that it would still be running 35 years later, but I am delighted that it is.

When I look back over the rich tapestry that is my business career, there is no doubt what I consider my favourite success. The Pizza Veneziana is undoubtedly my proudest working achievement.

27
CELEBRATING SOHO'S
SPLENDOUR: KETTNER'S

In 1980, I was at a function with the 'King of Soho' Paul Raymond, a multi-millionaire real estate developer who seemed to own half of the borough (including the country's first strip club).

Paul, who was a good friend of mine, had told me that he had grown tired of running Kettner's and asked if I was interested in taking it over. I don't remember what I was drinking at the time, but I would surely have spat it out in excitement at the opportunity.

Kettner's was the biggest restaurant in Soho, both in terms of its remarkable history and its four-storey building. It had been running on 29 Romilly Street since the 1860s, and to put it into perspective was named after its former head chef there Gustaf Kettner, who was Napoleon Bonaparte's cook. It was one of Oscar Wilde's favourite places to visit, and was home to numerous dates where the future King Edward VII would romance prospective lovers.

This was a restaurant of great splendour, garnished to the rafters with remarkable trinkets, but it had fallen into disarray in recent years. Paul was many things – including being a self-described 'porn baron' – but he was not a good restaurant owner. Despite Kettner's undoubted quality, it had sadly become a bit run down.

Even their most regular customers hadn't gone in for years, and the fear from Paul was that unless somebody could get the restaurant up and running it would be replaced by some tacky chain.

The thought of Kettner's becoming somewhere that a waiter dressed as a pirate serves you the daily 'buy one, get on free' cheeseburger specials filled us both with repulsion. This was still a landmark restaurant that any businessman worth his salt would love to own. I felt with a fresh menu (and a lick of paint), Kettner's could again be a place where actors and artisans would flock.

I agreed to buy the place for a modest fee, and decided to retain it as Kettner's rather than making it another PizzaExpress out of respect to Paul's hatred of chains. I bought it under the umbrella of 'Peter Boizot Franchise Ltd', a newly formed company that ran completely separately from PizzaExpress.

Despite agreeing not to turn it into a chain restaurant, I still leant heavily on tricks I had learnt at PizzaExpress.

The idea was to serve 'downmarket' food and 'upmarket' drinks – pizza and champagne, as I put it. To keep with the overall swanky feel, I wanted to not just restore the beauty of Kettner's, but to add to it.

I kept the wood-panelled reception area, but put in a door to the left with completely refitted champagne bar, which ate into half of the mirrored gold, red and cream coloured dining room, which also housed a magnificent painting of Gustaf Kettner.

This ground-floor divide halved the seating capacity, but I felt it would breathe new life into the place. The restaurant operated on a strict no-booking policy, and I wanted to retain that – but I also wanted to make it a place people were happy to queue while waiting to get into.

To create this veneer, I simply put a piano and accompanying pianist in the waiting area. He was Matt Ross – a skilled musician despite the handicap of being totally blind. He would belt out show tunes and gentle jazz on which could be heard in the street outside and attract people in.

Matt also had a fantastic trick of picking up familiar steps and voices in the room, and paid the person a compliment by incorporating a suitable theme tune into the piece he was playing. It's amazing how well simple tricks like this work in restaurants, and indeed people flocked inside to hear him like Odysseus being tempted by the sirens.

Once inside, they were happy to wait a few minutes while a seat was found for them – even if the restaurant was empty. A little waiting made the customer feel that being inside the restaurant was a treat in itself.

After they had been ushered through to their seat, they were faced with a two huge windows that stretched from ceiling to the floorboards which breathed life into the room. Above them were chandeliers, while laurel wreathes hung on the walls. There were 100 tables – including seats on pink banquettes that stretched around the walls in a style similar to Enzo's PizzaExpress layout.

In the middle of the room were rows of long tables with 16 seats around them – perfect for a birthday party. The second and third floors were painted in duck egg blue and silver. Customers perched on the tall stools or lounged at the tables dotted around.

I had a passion for paintings and drawings, and the rooms were decked with every size and type of art, some of which were created especially for the restaurant by Enzo.

My idea for the food was to merge high quality drinks with cheap fast food. So you could order £100 bottles of champagne to go with a cheap pizza. A lot of people had reservations about this approach, but it was in the heart of Soho – the home of London's film, music and television industries. I felt they would welcome the purposefully contradictory cheap food and expensive drinks with the curiosity that a creative mind possesses.

We reopened with a bang – dozens of celebrities were invited to see what the rebranded Kettner's was all about. I approached the paparazzi gathered outside and asked them if they wanted to come inside – I was sure they could get better photographs sitting in the lobby while the pianist tinkled the ivories.

That way, it would show the inside of the restaurant better and the celebrities would look calmer in the photographs. With a better picture, I assumed it would get a more prominent place in the newspaper. With a more prominent place in the paper, I hoped it would serve as a better advertisement.

The party was a smash hit and received rave reviews from the customers. It was held on a Friday night, and after I had shaken off my hangover for long enough to get to the shop, I was disappointed to see that we had not made the Saturday papers.

Despite the healthy turnout of celebrities and the paparazzi, not a single photograph had appeared in the national press. This was a disappointment, but not enough to shake the feeling of success from the night before. I was looking forward to the second night at the restaurant later that evening.

Saturday night came and went in a blur, and then on Sunday I received a phone call from my mother up in Peterborough. She said that she had seen my restaurant in the Sunday paper. I ran down to the shop and picked up the *News of The World*, and there was Kettner's in the gossip pages. I looked through the Sunday Mirror, and there we were again! Next *The Sunday Mail*, then *The Sunday Times* – Kettner's was in each and every one.

I learnt two lessons – first, celebrities only call photographers paparazzi if they are hounding them outside. Invite them into the establishment, where the model can pose in calm surroundings, and suddenly these camera-holding 'parasites' become professional photographers.

The second lesson was that if a party is *really* good, you won't read about it in the next day's newspaper.

I had phoned one of the photographers, who had given me his card, and asked why it was in the Sunday papers rather than the Saturday editions. He gave some pithy response that Sunday is more gossip-orientated than Saturday, but I felt that was a little hard to understand.

After all, when I worked at the Associated Press in Rome, the editor would say that 'news is news', there was no such thing as 'Saturday news' and 'Sunday news'.

Once pressed, the photographer laughed and admitted that he and his peers had ditched their equipment in the cloakroom and sauntered into the Champagne Bar, and had made a pact not to sell their photographs until the next afternoon so they could enjoy the night and not have to wake up early in the morning.

The fact they were able to hide within that packed Champagne Bar was a good indicator that people would cram into a place with posh drinks, even if it was also where common food was served. And that fact was re-enforced every Friday and Saturday night for the next few months!

Kettner's quickly became the celebrity hot-spot of central London. You couldn't move for people, and you also couldn't pick up a copy of one of the national gossip magazines without seeing my restaurant within its glossy pages. Of course, the restaurant was always in the background of a picture of the latest footballer or musician – and it all helped to raise our profile.

I heard that PR gurus like Max Clifford would recommend stars to go there at least once a month to keep their faces in the paper. That meant more and more people would see the place, and more and more money would come my way.

Undoubtedly the most high-profile customer we had was Lady Diana Spencer, the soon-to-be Princess of

Wales. Diana came to Kettner's the winter before she married into the Royal Family with her future sister-in-law, Princess Anne.

Princess Anne was a regular customer, who I had briefly met before, but to my knowledge Diana only came in once. Sadly, when she did, I was on a tomato-finding exercise in Italy. Such is the bane of having multiple jobs at once. But Diana's trip to Kettner's was, inevitably, picked up by all the newspapers.

It wasn't my only brush with the monarchy, for whom I hold an immense admiration. In the late 1980s, Prince Charles held a large party in Hyde Park. I sent Buckingham Palace a case of a few dozen champagne glasses from our bar out of respect for the Royal Family. I also sent a few bottles of champagne along with a note saying that I hoped the Prince could hand out a few drinks to the lucky attendees in the park.

A very touching letter came back from the Palace to say that the donation was greatly appreciated by the Prince – and I'd like to think the revellers who got a free glass of bubbly enjoyed it as well.

One celebrity that I did see while in the restaurant was Marlon Brando. I was sitting in the Champagne Bar with a group of friends from the Hampstead Hockey Club when there was an almighty cacophony in the hallway. I poked my head through the door, and standing there was none other than Don Vito Corleone.

Brando had been criticised by some Italians for his portrayal of the head of a family of mobsters in *The Godfather*. The film, based on a Mario Puzo novel of the same name, had been released in 1972, and had been described varyingly as the most accurate portrayal of the mafia or a disproportionate exaggeration of fictional crime rings.

As such, its star divided opinion amongst Italians. But before I could introduce myself and make my own judgement, my old friend Renée Brittain ran over from the restaurant side and gave him a big hug and an even bigger kiss on the cheek! I later learnt that they had met at some party in London a few days earlier, and got on like a house on fire.

The next thing I knew, she ushered Brando out of the door onto Romilly Street and then whisked him away in her 2CV. I was disappointed not to have had the chance to entertain this Hollywood icon in my restaurant, but I couldn't stay mad at Renée. After all, she had grasped the opportunity to drive around London with the world's biggest film star – who could blame her?

Although Brando didn't stay for long, it still proved yet again that Kettner's had a magnetic pull on celebrities. The publicity of getting seen in my restaurant helped to boost many careers, and in doing so, also boosted our own takings by getting us in the newspapers.

The circle of life!

28
THE ULTIMATE WING MAN

A year after I bought Kettner's, I was truly blessed to find the man who helped take so much pressure off me running PizzaExpress – and would also become one of my closest friends. In the Easter of 1981, I met Robert 'Dickie' Bird.

When I look back on it, I can scarcely believe PizzaExpress ran for so long without him. He was an integral cog, and it feels very strange that we ran for 16 years without him. Peter Boizot running PizzaExpress without Dickie Bird feels rather like Batman looking after Gotham City without Robin – just not right.

Early on in 1981, I made the decision to bring in a Food Quality Controller. Amongst the expansion and the branding of the company, I was worried that the standard of the food was not quite up to scratch. Everything was going well, but I feared that decreasing standards would create a gap in our armour, and the whole reputation of PizzaExpress would fall down like a deck of cards. Food first, everything else second.

Against other people's advice I put an advert into Hotel and Catering Magazine for people with 'technical background', preferably in baking and cake making. Others on the board felt this would look desperate – they thought a big company like PizzaExpress should headhunt the right person. They felt putting an advert in a magazine opened the door for any old Tom, Dick or Harry to apply.

In the end, a Dick did apply and he turned out to be the perfect candidate.

My thinking for putting it in the magazine was that I wanted to unearth a gem. A diamond in the rough. Sometimes ability does not keep up with circumstances, and throughout the country there are thousands of people with ample ability but denied that opportunity to break through. I wanted that sort of person. I wanted the people who had toiled, scraped and mastered their trade, and would now appreciate a break at a bigger company.

At the time, Dickie Bird was working as a mobile chef for banks in the city. He started baking cakes in the early 1960s, had worked in food labs and then became a test baker for flour millers. His CV was solid if unspectacular, and to be honest didn't jump out of the list of applicants. I would later learn that this was due to his modesty, which is another highly admirable trait.

I invited Dickie and another applicant to interview for the job. The interview would have two parts – practical and personal. Practical, because I wanted to know they knew more about food than anyone currently at PizzaExpress did (and hence were worth employing), and personal because I didn't want to bring anyone into our family who might rock the boat.

The interview took place in the Dean Street PizzaExpress. The applicants should have known something was suspect from the scenery, but they had no idea what to expect.

Both candidates people thought they were the only candidate being interviewed for the job – that way, you can see how they are when they are relaxed. If they were complacent, they're not the right candidate for this job. If they were focused, it would show they were disciplined, self-motivated and competitive.

The first candidate was a jolly young woman from the north of England. Heavy-set on a small frame, she certainly looked like she was no stranger to a full dinner plate. But this isn't a bad thing for somebody in the food industry, and she had the most impressive credentials of the three, having worked as a chef in a top restaurant and then subsidised her earnings as a critic for the Michelin Guide.

The second applicant was a man who was around 30 years old, blessed with a natural charm and presence that belied his young age. He dressed smartly with thick-rimmed glasses that lay on a thick head of hair. It was the previously mentioned mobile chef known as 'Dickie' Bird – not to be confused with the cricket umpire of the same name.

The first thing I did to greet the candidates in the interview was wheel out a food tray with two dishes in it – chocolate cake and tomato soup.

The first was a fabulous product; the second was routine to a lay person but exquisite to an expert. The trick was to see if they could identify the herb put in the tomato soup – three leaves of basil. Any Food Quality Controller worth their salt would recognise that, so I thought it was a good barometer.

The rotund female applicant's eyes widened when the interview started with a food tray being wheeled into the room. They almost popped out of their sockets when the sheet was removed to expose a chocolate cake! She ate it, and I asked her what she thought of it. Full of praise and the sort of magnificent adjectives one would expect from a food reviewer.

Then it was onto the tomato soup. Again, she dived in and helped herself, and again she came back with a rapturously positive appraisal.

I asked her to explain why the tomato soup was so impressive. She came back with a somewhat disingenuous reply of the taste hitting the back of her throat and leaving an unforgettable taste, or some such generic codswallop.

I asked what it was that gave the taste – she just said the tomato. This was a most unimpressive answer. She didn't even guess at a herb, let alone identify it as basil.

She had all the enthusiasm in the world, but she struck me more of a lover of food than a true critic of it. The Food Quality Controller would have to call a spade a spade (and a rum pizza a rum pizza). I didn't even bother with the personal interview questions.

I thanked her for her time, and told her we would be in touch – knowing, all the while, that we wouldn't. My gut feelings told me that she would not hold PizzaExpress up to the tightest of scrutiny. My gut told me she wouldn't benefit our business. I make decisions with my gut and, fortunately for me, my gut has been good to me over the years.

Next came Dickie. He seemed endearingly nervous – clearly trying his best to impress and land the job. As such, he almost fell out of his seat when I wheeled in the tray – that was the last thing he was expecting.

First I told him to eat the chocolate cake. It was a truly fabulous product, and the enthusiasm Dickie gave me after eating it made me realise he had the necessary passion for food.

Next came the all-important tomato soup. Dickie grabbed a spoon and dived into the bowl. After one mouthful, and without even a moment's pushing, he looked at me and said, "Is that basil?" I was impressed.

But I thought I'd tease him, and incredulously asked, "You can taste... *basil*?"

Unflustered, Dickie fixed a look in my eye and calmly said, "Yes – most likely three leaves."

Bingo!

Not only had he correctly identified the scarce scent of the herb, but he maintained that he was correct despite my exaggerated pretence that he was wrong. He even guessed the number of leaves used to make the soup! This was most impressive.

I immediately thrust into the second half of the interview – the personal questions. Dickie told me that he had always loved cooking and took a job as a pot washer a few years earlier.

One day the young chef needed to make a cake and he said he wasn't very confident at making cakes, so Dickie volunteered. Impressed with his confidence (and given the chance to pass on a job), the chef put faith in the pot washer and let him bake the cake.

A short while later, the chef returned and saw that Dickie had baked a fantastic cake with no problem. The chef, in his wisdom, immediately took Dickie off pot washing duty and said, "You're on starters and desserts." That chef, incidentally, was Anthony Worrell-Thompson, who would go on to be one of the most respected in the business and even a popular television personality.

Again, I was impressed. When I'm conducting an interview I look for their ability, potential and likeability. This story showed that Dickie had all three. The taste test showed this was the right job for him. After I thanked him for coming, my mind was made up – this was our new Food Quality Controller.

Three weeks passed by and I was sitting doing some paperwork in my office above Dean Street when the phone rang. An exasperated voice on the other end of the line said, "Mr Boizot, I haven't heard anything from you in three weeks and I am driving the postman crazy asking him if he's seen a letter from you."

I recognised the voice, though not its tone. I asked, "Is that you Dickie? You start on Monday. My secretary must have forgotten to send the letter out."

I think he realised that the mistake was not down to my poor old secretary, but I had simply forgotten to bottom out the deal. I was so confident that we had found the perfect Food Quality Controller that I put the whole matter to the back of my mind – and totally forgot to tell the person who I wanted to fill the job!

When told at dinner parties, such stories are often met with howls of laughter from men who share my condition, and furrowed brows from women no doubt wondering how I got to be a businessman in charge of thousands of employees!

He started off at the Notting Hill Gate branch and was told to learn everything about making pizzas. What better way to fully understand an industry than work in it? Dickie took to it like a duck to water, and was soon upgraded to the slightly more prestigious title of 'Quality Assurance Director', and since the turn of the 21st century has worked as a consultant to a wide range of businesses as a pizza expert.

Dickie also went on to help man my humorously named 'Outside Catering Division', along with another capable man named Richard Balkwell. At my request, they stood outside St Catharine's College for the May Ball. While there, they would hand out free pizzas to the revellers as they stumbled out from the debauchery of the ball. They would bring up hundreds of pizzas that were three-quarters cooked and hand them out. It was a real hoot – great fun.

I made Dickie and Richard wear smart clothes and bowties, which was a bit of a rib because by the end of the day they would be covered in flour and tomatoes.

I felt such frivolities were good for publicity and also morale. The first time we did it was in the mid-1980s and I remember Dickie was a little unsure about the initiative. He asked what the other directors would say about it all – I turned and said, "I know I have got other directors but I don't have to listen to them."

Dickie and I had many fantastic nights out in Soho. I remember often leaving the Wardour Street restaurant at 6pm, and he would want to get back home to his family. But I would always say, "Where are you going – surely you can stay for a drink?"

The next thing you knew, we were both propping up lamp posts at 11pm chatting to everybody who walked past. The regular repetition of such occurrences was probably indicative of my life without a wife.

Yet despite our close friendship, it was a full 20 years until Dickie called me 'Peter'. We went all over Europe together, but he would still always call him 'Mr Boizot'. One day, I just said, "Come on Dickie, I think you should be calling me Peter". Calling me 'Mr Boizot' was intended as a sign of respect from a bygone age, and it spoke a lot about Dickie as a man and the code he lived by. I felt honoured by it at first, but as the years turned into decades (and our friendship grew ever stronger) I thought it was time to be a little less formal.

Going back to my earlier analogy, you would never hear Bruce Wayne's sidekick Robin call out for 'Mr Batman'!

CHAPTER VI:
ENJOYING MY SUCCESS

While you are waiting for the pizza to be ready, tidy up all the apparatus that you used to make it. This might get a little bit messy, but it's an important step – you will be so full after eating your banquet that you won't want to touch the dishes.

Similarly, in life you cannot just sit back and wait for good things to come to you – you have to put plans in place to make sure what you want to happen comes to fruition.

Even if sometimes the vision you have is not shared by others, you have to stay resolute and continue preparing the world for the changes you want to happen.

29
MOVING UP IN THE WORLD, BUT HELPING OTHERS ONTO THEIR FEET

After Dickie Bird joined, PizzaExpress finally felt complete. And by 1983, I had a similar feeling of contentment in my personal life – I really felt I was an established member of the London elite.

I moved into a luxurious new house on Lowndes Square, in Belgravia, central London. The square is in the shadow of Knightsbridge and Sloane Square, and within a walk-of-a-corgi from Buckingham Palace. So as you can imagine it is home to some of the most expensive properties in the world – one of which is now owned by Russian billionaire Roman Abramovic.

Lowndes Square is characterised by its grand terraces with white stucco houses, but my flat was a smaller brown brick building just off the Square. When I moved in, I inevitably held a party to introduce myself to my neighbours, who flocked to meet the new kid on the block.

I was delighted to see that amongst my neighbours was an elderly relative of Poly, Earl of Norbury, my old chum who was so instrumental in the creation of PizzaExpress. She had been told of Poly's links to the company, and was similarly excited to gain my acquaintance. We quickly became good friends, and I helped to run errands she needed help with, such as shopping or giving her a lift when she needed to get somewhere.

I never took to the London Underground (or 'Tube'), and hated the idea of friends going on it. I felt claustrophobic travelling along in a jolting, sideways fashion underneath the sewers, and it was incomprehensively hot and stuffy. I always preferred driving in my own car, and felt by comparison using the Tube was akin to scrambling underground like a rat. For that reason, I only ever used the Underground twice, and also always insisted on offering friends lifts in my car if they needed to get anywhere.

Through such lifts, a friendship with Poly's relative was struck up, but then all too quickly, she passed away. I didn't know her too well to truly grieve, but it was an incredibly sad situation. What came as an even bigger surprise was the fact that in her will, she had decided to leave her flat to me.

That meant that I now had two flats on Lowndes Square. The one I inherited was one of the huge white buildings that overlook the park in the middle of the square. I have always lived on my own, but now had two houses for one person – and yet I spent most of my time in the office on Dean Street, anyway.

I was delighted with the flats, and they helped me to truly enjoy my time away from work. One time I had the pleasure of a delightful young Danish girl come to visit me, one of my many girlfriends at the time (whose name I will withhold in the name of chivalry).

She told me she was going to leave my house and walk a couple of miles to Covent Garden, so I inevitably offered to walk her there. On our way to town, we approached a Rolls-Royce dealership. The girl squealed with Scandinavian stimulation about this most British of sights, and said how she would buy a Rolls-Royce but for two obstacles – her lack of money, and her lack of a driving licence.

Never one to miss a trick, I asked her if she would come back to visit me if I had a Rolls-Royce. She giggled as if to say, "I would, but it won't happen" – and so I took her by the hand and walked into the dealership. Thirty minutes later, I drove out with an almost brand new car... and a very happy girlfriend.

Whenever she came to visit, we would take the Rolls out for a spin, and I enjoyed riding it very much. But after we inevitably split up, the car sat dormant in my garage. When a friend pointed out that it had been locked up for 12 weeks without spinning a wheel, I realised that the whole situation had become somewhat ridiculous and decided to sell the car. Co-incidentally, the man who bought it came from Stilton, not 10 miles from Peterborough. I just hope it held up to the challenges posed by the rustic roads of rural Cambridgeshire!

It was while walking with Dickie in Soho that I also created another questionable yet treasured business habit – offering jobs to the homeless.

We were on our way from Kettner's to the Wardour Street PizzaExpress when we bumped into a homeless man. I noticed him while we walked down the street – dishevelled with a three-day-old hangover, a three-week beard and three-year-old clothes. There was nothing spectacular about this homeless man; he was the sort of person you can see in any city centre on any day of the week.

But perhaps it was because I was coming from Kettner's, a place of great wealth and splendour, that I felt an emotional pang towards this poor soul. It was relentlessly unfair that some (myself included) could enjoy a lavish lifestyle, while others had to scrape by in poverty.

Inevitably, the man approached me with an outstretched polystyrene cup, and asked me if I could spare any change. Walking between two of my restaurants while wearing a fashionable three-piece suit, it was quite obvious that I *could* afford to give him some money. The important question was *would* I give him some money?

I turned to him and said, "I don't give money to people like you", which would have disappointed the homeless man, but was no doubt something he would have heard numerous times before. However, I wasn't finished.

"I won't give you money here in the street, but I can give you a job. You can come and be a pot washer in my restaurant. And if you do that job well, you will get a lot of money from me, rather than just some change in the street."

I had never thought of this before, but like divine inspiration it came to me in a flash. This way, I could redistribute money to the homeless, give them an opportunity, and also get some new employees in.

The chap was most excited by my offer and agreed to take the job. I asked when he could start, and he said straight away. I told him that he couldn't come into our kitchen until he'd had a shave and a shower, but that a change of clothes and a j-cloth would be waiting for him.

The very next morning he appeared fit and raring to go. I shall keep his name out of the book, because he very quickly turned into a man who you would never think had slept rough in his life. His life has changed around so much that I do not know if his friends and family know of the period when he was on tough times.

But that man who took his chance as a pot washer soon moved onto a higher pay grade as a waiter in the restaurant, before leaving to set up his own auction house. Within a few years of being given that opportunity he had done so well for himself that he could afford to buy a house in London.

Anyone who knows the housing market in the capital knows that constitutes quite the turnaround after he grasped that first opportunity.

However, despite his successes, for many years he still returned to PizzaExpress to help with our washing up because he felt he owed it to me for giving him that chance. I always felt a little bit embarrassed by this – I was only doing what my priests had told me to do for decades, and I was after all benefiting from his services.

But I still think that it is a magnificent story, and one that I hope inspires others to help people who are down on their luck. Who knows what potential lies on the street at night?

After this 'Road to Damascus' moment, I vowed to never walk past another homeless person without offering them the same thing. I can't count how many people I had this conversation with over the next decade.

Some grasped the offer with two hands and took the job, which meant they could then get on the housing register and sign up with a doctor. Sadly, many declined the offer outright. Others would turn up for one or two shifts and then never appear again. But I think the onus is on you to do something good for somebody else – how they use that distribution of goodwill is up to them.

There was another time when I was in Germany on a trip to look into sausage meat with Dickie that another homeless person stopped me in the street, asking for money. I could not offer this poor soul a job, because I did not own a restaurant in Germany.

However, I could offer him an experience. With a smattering of German and relying heavily on hand gestures, I invited him to join Dickie and I in the Bavarian tavern we were walking next to. The homeless man took us up on our offer, and in no time we had him sat on our table with a glass of cider and a packet of the bar's most expensive cigars, talking about my previous life selling encyclopaedias in Germany (although I'm not sure how much he understood).

I think you can judge a society on how it treats its most vulnerable people. I wish we could do more to help our homeless people, but it seems to be a perpetual problem that may never find a permanent solution.

30
SWINGING SWINDON (AND OTHER SQUABBLES)

The PizzaExpress franchise was a rather strange necklace. All the parts were autonomous, but there was still a guiding influence from me. The business model in each branch was the same, although each had their own managers.

This created something of a family, but none of the people in it were actually related. Although the system seemed to work rather well most of the time, it did create with it some problems, which with hindsight may have been headaches for my franchisees.

A good way of describing the dichotomy between the franchises and I came through the simple act of carrying a pair of scissors with me whenever I went into a branch. The reason for this was because I always wanted the restaurants to look clean and tidy, and I felt the way a manager kept their flowers symbolised the care and attention they gave to their branch.

And so, if I felt a flower was too prominent, I would simply remove it from the vase, and snip it to an appropriate length.

On many occasions, I wandered into a PizzaExpress, be it in Leicester or Sheffield or wherever, and walked around the branch snipping the flowers while the exasperated franchisee looked on. Dickie told me that they thought it was a way of exerting power; of saying that 'you may be the franchisee but I am still the manager'. But I never thought of it like that – I just didn't want the restaurant to look messy.

The best analogy for the grey lines within the franchise came with a new restaurant we opened in the mid-1980s. After seeing the great successes of Kettner's, I decided that I wanted a similar feel at a PizzaExpress. A wine bar within a pizzeria.

When the next franchisee came around, it was a gentleman from Swindon. I had known very little of Swindon, so I made a trip to see the proposed site. The town reminded me rather of my hometown of Peterborough, albeit slightly more industrial and grey.

Swindon sat midway between two large conurbations in Bristol and Reading, while Peterborough was the halfway point between Cambridge and Leicester. Both were around 80 miles from London, and had similar population sizes and demographics. Blue collar workers.

These comparisons led me to a natural affinity with Swindon, and I decided that this should be the place where the PizzaExpress wine bar should be housed. I gave the nod to the franchisee to go ahead with the branch on one condition – that the entire first floor should be a swanky champagne bar.

I went along to the launch night, and was delighted that the great and the good from Swindon turned out to see how pizza and champagne would mix in their hometown. It was a well-attended, lavish affair, and I left contented that the people of Swindon would make the most of their new establishment.

It was a magnificent building – a near replica of what we had in Kettner's. Every person who approached me said that it was unlike anything they had in Swindon, and thanked me for adding a little glitz and glamour to their city centre. The restaurant and bar overlooked a rather grim 1970s shopping centre, and I felt it would create a nice 'diamond in the rough' (no offence intended at all to the good people of Swindon).

However, the short-term success of that night did not transfer off after I returned to London. The profit returns were sent through to me every month, and the branch was always losing money. The PizzaExpress was doing well, but overall money was being lost because the wine bar was causing so much financial damage.

I phoned the franchisee, and said that perhaps Swindon would simply take a bit of time getting used to the style of the wine bar. But I assured him that it would take off. With a population of over 100,000, in time it would be the place to hold birthday or work parties – or even wedding receptions. In the meantime, I told him I would subsidise the champagne bar with money belonging to PizzaExpress Ltd.

I also decided to buy a magnificent modern sculpture to put outside the building to attract interest. It was called 'The Spirit of Brunel' and had been made by the internationally famous artist Eduardo Paolozzi (who I would later be privileged enough to call my friend).

I felt it would be fitting for the restaurant in Swindon, because its muse Isambard Kingdom Brunel had pioneered the Great Western Railway, whose locomotives were built in workshops in Swindon.

This addition was another contradiction with the mantra of "a good restaurant needs no bush" – I'm afraid to say that, once again, it appeared that people would never see that restaurant unless there was a bush to attract them.

However, it didn't work. The deficits continued and it lost money every month that it was open. At one annual general meeting of all the franchisees, I remember a gentleman who ran a very profitable modest restaurant in London took umbrage at the situation in Swindon.

After I praised the franchisees on another fantastic year in business, this chap stood up and said, "Well why don't you just send our profits in an envelope to Swindon? That is what you have been doing for the last couple of years!"

It was a little bit embarrassing, but I could not change the way I ran my business. For better or worse, I was loyal to all employees and committed to all ventures. I was determined to help the champagne bar to succeed.

Quitting was not an option.

I have often said that the key success for my business ventures has been sheer bloody mindedness and having total faith in my decisions. I regret to say that the very attributes that brought me success were also my Achilles' heel.

As the other franchisees said, that champagne bar in Swindon lost the whole company money every week of the three years that it was open. I have heard rumours that the franchisee put on karaoke nights and 'drinks half price for ladies' events, which I have always abhorred, and maybe that didn't help create the veneer of a sophisticated establishment.

After three years of struggling along (and being propped up by the parent company's subsidies), the franchisee decided to close down the restaurant. I chose to ship all the champagne bar materials back to Kettner's, and gave up on the dream of having it in Swindon. In time, another PizzaExpress opened on Bath Street, Swindon, and has run very well ever since – albeit, without any champagne bars.

Another problem with a branch we had was a little restaurant on Wembley High Street. It was not a mover – mainly because of the ethnic distribution of the area, which was populated with Indian families who would rather have a curry than a pizza.

The others in the company were forever telling me to close the Wembley branch, because it was a drain on money for the rest of the group. If one restaurant struggled, all the other branches felt the financial pinch as well.

This all came to a head when we had the annual Christmas party in the basement of the Wardour Street branch. People were sniping at me all night to close the blessed restaurant down and call a loss a loss.

After a few too many remarks (and probably a few too many drinks), I stood on a chair to address my peers. I stated, quite passionately, that I am not in the business of closing restaurants. I told them that they ought to be ashamed of themselves for politicking me to do so, and reminded them that maybe one day they would come to rely on my patient nature as a boss.

It was a pride thing – I didn't want to admit we had made a mistake opening in that area. But at the same time, I wanted to prove a point to my franchisees. When they joined the PizzaExpress family, they were with us for life. It was not a matter of cutting that family member off as soon as there was a problem.

Another restaurant my employees wanted me to close down did not even belong to me. It was a small takeaway which, like the Greek waiter who created a PizzaExpress in Athens, was stealing from our business model – but had the temerity to do it on our doorstep in London.

Dickie came running into my office on Dean Street one time and said that he had been walking down Kensington High Street and seen a small pizzeria called 'PizzaExpress' opposite Barkers. He popped his head in the door and this takeaway pizza joint had the cheek of not only stealing our name – but also our menu. It was a photocopy of the sheets we would put on the tables.

Dickie said that I must take legal action, but my reaction was similar to the one I had after learning of the Greek's swindle – "Doesn't it make you proud that people want to copy us?", I asked my loyal employee.

Eventually, after much persuasion from Dickie and others, I got a lawyer to write them a letter asking them to stop. But I never pursued it – my head was not screwed on for business, it was screwed on for pizza. I didn't want to make enemies with somebody who simply wanted to sell pizzas – after all, by that logic the Italians could have me in on a tribunal for stealing their national dish.

One other bone of contention within the company that I would always like to address is why we never had a PizzaExpress in my beloved hometown of Peterborough while I was in charge. There were plenty of offers, but I always turned them down.

Over the years I have heard all sorts of embellished rumours about that, but the real reason is far less sensationalist than others may have you believe.

Some think I wanted Peterborough as my 'escape' from PizzaExpress. Firstly, this is nonsense for the basic reason that I have been well known in my home city for years (including the Parliamentary campaigns), so the idea that I could down tools and rest away from the hustle and bustle of London in the anonymity of Peterborough is nonsense.

Secondly, anybody who knows me will tell you that I thrive on being recognised. I love talking to people and have an affection for being in the limelight. I love a good party and I love a good pizza. Creating a franchise in Peterborough would tick all of those boxes.

The real reason for not opening the restaurant was simple: there were too many Italians in Peterborough. The city was crammed full of them!

Peterborough became a magnet for Italian migration in the 1950s, when the London Brick Company advertised jobs in the city to people from Puglia and Campania. This was long after I had moved out of my parents' home, but as a regular visitor I noticed their presence simply grew and grew.

I was fearful that they would notice that our pizzas were not made in ovens built to the top, authentic, Italian standard. I was worried that PizzaExpress would be labelled a 'rip-off' by the people who had come over in the 1950s and 1960s from the dish's motherland.

My directors would forever push me to open a branch in Peterborough. You could see their logic – we sold Italian food, there were lots of Italians in Peterborough, Italians like pizza, I was from Peterborough. It became something of a long-running joke how proud I was of my hometown, yet refused to open a branch there. My colleagues even started to call me *'Mr Pizzaborough'* – a fitting name, but ironic when considered in this context.

Try as I might, I just couldn't shake the feeling that Italian diners would not be impressed with my restaurant. Although I was proud of the food we made, I never ate a pizza in a PizzaExpress restaurant that was as good as a pizza I ate in Italy.

I would never tell anyone the real reason for not opening a restaurant in Peterborough. Not my friends, colleagues or even relatives. I would flippantly say, "Oh, there's only so many places we have PizzaExpress restaurants. I'm sure we will get around to it" – but secretly, I knew it would never happen on my watch.

So there is a big Peter Boizot secret – the reason PizzaExpress never opened in Peterborough while I was well-and-truly holding the company's reigns was simply because there were too many authentic Italians in the city!

I think the way I see the world is different to the way a lot of my franchisees saw it. I am not a cold-blooded, money-driven businessman. My decisions have been driven by opinion and passion rather than looking at figures. For example, in 1984 I decided that every pizzaiolo in a PizzaExpress must wear a hat. It cost us a surprising amount of money and many of the franchisees argued that no customer had ever expressed concern at the hygiene of the chefs.

But it wasn't a question of hygiene – it was a question of appearances. I felt a hat adds a level of uniform to the operation and makes a chef quite authoritative. It sets them apart from the other employees like the number of stripes on a policeman's sleeve.

This opinion was laughed at by the other franchisees – until they adopted it in their restaurants and the new smart look received nothing but plaudits.

I made some decisions that they would think to be rather strange. But I think those decisions that they perceived as being 'bizarre' more often than not turned out to be the right ones. And I'm still cantankerous enough to think the ones that didn't work out would have done if given a little more time.

31
AWARDS AND RECOGNITION

In October 1983, I was going through the mail in my Dean Street office when a letter jumped out at me – it was stamped with the authoritative logo of the Italian Government.

Of course, when one gets a letter from the government there is one thing that flashes into one's mind: what have I done wrong? Maybe they had finally cottoned on to the 'Caesar's horseshoe' trick I was pulling on tourists in Rome, and wanted to hold me to task!

I fervently opened the letter and was shocked and delighted at its contents. I had been awarded the decoration of 'Cavaliere Ufficiale, al Merito Della Repubblica Italiana'. *Cavaliere* is Italian for 'Knight' – the equivalent of a British knighthood.

I could not have been prouder. From being a skinny, wide-eyed teenager who had been embraced by the country in 1948 to being given the equivalent of a knighthood. It was a magnificent thrill. I quickly called the Italian Embassy in London and said that I would of course be delighted to accept the honour.

The voice on the other end of the telephone explained to me that the status of *Cavaliere Ufficiale* was given for outstanding merit in regard to the nation of Italy. It had been bestowed upon me due to the success of the Pizza Veneziana, which by that point had raised £600,000 for the Venice In Peril Fund – well on the way to the £2 million plus it has raised now.

By that point, it had already paid for countless restoration projects, including the Capella Amiliani on the island of San Michele and the Porta della Carta at the Doge's Palace. After learning the news, I phoned some friends and hastily organised a bash to celebrate the news – fittingly, it was at PizzaExpress and we celebrated by eating pizzas and drinking Peroni into the wee hours of the night. How the Italian forefathers who laid the path for the great nation would have been proud!

The honour doesn't mean much in terms of what I can do – as far as I know, I can't walk sheep through the streets of Venice (a bizarre right that is given to people given the Freedom of English cities). But being Cavaliere Boizot is something that I hold in great esteem. One interesting quirk that did come with my newly found social status was that I could now sign off my letters with "cav. uff" after my name. I did so at first, but quickly stopped because I grew tired of people asking me what the letters meant.

I feared that it may appear that I was just adding the 'cav. uff' signature to invite that question. That felt incredibly egotistical, and out of respect for the honour I actually stopped putting it at the end of my letters. The phrase 'empty vessels make the most noise' comes to mind – and I felt it was more fitting with a *Cavaliere* to be modest about the achievement than use it as some sort of a prop for an egotistical conversation starter.

Just a month after I was made a *Cavaliere Ufficiale*, I received another award for my services to Venice. Obviously my name was doing the rounds with the chattering classes. And so, in November 1983 I was given the 'Bolla Award' – a presentation given annually to the British person considered to have done the most for

Venice that year. It was a rather ostentatious award, and one that I felt should be given to the patrons of the Venice In Peril Fund every year. But, any publicity for the cause is good publicity, and I gratefully accepted the award.

It was given to me by the Chancellor of the Exchequer, Nigel Lawson, whose daughter Nigella has, of course, since gone on to have made quite a splash in the culinary world herself. The photograph of me accepting the award from the MP appeared in numerous glossy magazines, most importantly with a bit of writing about the perils Venice still faced. I understand that it was also syndicated to Italy and was printed in some of their newspapers. It pleased me immensely that their citizens could see that this man making money from their national dish was doing his best to help the country.

While I was immensely proud of this recognition, it could not compare with one my feelings created by another honour that was bestowed on me a couple of years later.

By 1986, PizzaExpress had given employment to hundreds, if not thousands, of people – ranging from executives on high salaries to students looking for some beer money by washing pots.

Quite unexpectedly, a letter arrived in the post addressed from Buckingham Palace. The note told me that, in recognition of the jobs I had created, I was to be given an MBE (Member of the Most Excellent Order of the British Empire.

I had a totally different feeling towards the MBE – granted for job creation – than I had for the Italian honours – given because of personal passions and moral pursuits. Being someone who had more than my fair share of jobs until I settled down in the mid-1960s, I had always respected job creators. Over the years, I had gradually become an employer of many hundreds of people – and with hindsight, I didn't really appreciate that until I got my MBE.

While my *Cavaliere Ufficiale* and Bella Award came from me giving away money – the MBE came from me creating opportunities for others to make money. That gave me a different kind of pride – as did the fact it was an honour bestowed by my own queen.

I decided to take my mother as my 'plus one'. On the morning of the big day, I set off from London at 6am and drove up to Peterborough to collect her. We then did a quick u-turn back to the capital, parked up at Lowndes Square and went to see the Queen. She was as proud as a peacock to see her little boy given an MBE, and having her in the audience made me even more happy to collect the honour.

The Queen was magnificent, both in conversation and appearance. She had clearly done her research before handing out all the awards, and had a small polite chat with each of the recipients. She may be three years older than me, but she looked a good 20 years younger, with a fair complexion, wrinkle-free face and brown hair (compared to mine, which was long-since greyed).

I would very much like to meet the Queen again, and have made no secret of my remaining dream being to be made a knight of the realm. I say this not just because I want to be introduced to people as 'Sir Peter Boizot', but also because I think it could inspire others to follow my entrepreneurial and philanthropic footsteps.

But saying that, I must confess that I believe 'Sir Peter Boizot' does have a rather nice ring to it!

Receiving my MBE from the Queen

32
THE SOHO JAZZ FESTIVAL

After gratefully receiving all these awards, I decided that I had earned the right to have a little bit more fun. I decided to combine two of my favourite things – the borough of Soho and the majesty of jazz music.

The popularity of the jazz club below the Dean Street pizzeria led my mind to wander about how this idea could be expanded further. It was fantastic that people were coming to listen to the performances, but the fact that they had to come to us meant it was only ever jazz fans listening to jazz music. What I wanted to do was bring the jazz performances to the general public.

I wanted jazz to take over Soho in the same way that comedy takes over Edinburgh every year for the Fringe Festival, and decided it would be a good idea to promote an event called the 'Soho Jazz and Heritage Festival'... although colloquially come to be known simply as the 'Soho Jazz Festival'.

The idea was to put on a fortnight-long celebration of music at the end of September and the start of October. I would help to book jazz musicians to appear all over Soho, for no financial benefit, in the hope that it would turn that little pocket of London into New Orleans for a couple of weeks.

At first, the festival was something of an ad-hoc affair. Of course, I booked as many musicians as possible for my restaurants, and also recommend jazz artists to other businesses associated to the Soho Society. I also put up banners in PizzaExpress branches and paid for advertising boards to be placed all over London to let people know that the 1986 Soho Jazz Festival was coming.

We put on events all over Soho (and sprawled out slightly into other boroughs as well). It wasn't just traditional jazz – one of the best reviewed gigs was by Marc Almond, who was the lead singer of famous pop band Soft Cell.

His solo show at the London Palladium at the inaugural Soho Jazz Festival was rated as one of the performances of the year by cult music magazine the *New Musical Express (NME)*. It wasn't only jazz music – we also had fabulous fun watching all the restaurants of Soho taking part in a waiters' race around the borough's streets.

The old salesman in me came to the fore as I shouted down a megaphone to gather the disorganised rabble to the start. Visitors crowded around the circuit through those old cobbled Soho streets, and I set the very well-dressed (and tray-carrying) waiters off from Old Compton Street.

The waiters were tasked to sprint through Soho's many twists and turns dressed in full uniform while holding a plate with their restaurant's specialist dish. This had been a tradition back in the 1950s that had sadly died out. Once re-introduced as part of the Soho Jazz Festival we had around 15 waiters turn out for the big day, and hundreds crowded the streets.

Most wanted to see a waiter slip over and end up with spaghetti on their face – and that's exactly what happened after one sprightly-heeled runner slipped while navigating a corner onto the home straight. If it was advertised more prominently, the Soho Waiters' Race could be bigger than the Grand National!

After the race, I would return to the church precincts where eating, drinking and merry making were the order of the day. The performers on stage ranged from drag acts like Ruby Venozailor to groups like The Elastic Band, to Noel Botham's hilarious Elvis Presley impression.

There were also silly competitions such as fancy dress and balloon bursting – often with me presiding over the competitions with a small Havana cigar in my mouth.

The festival snowballed instantly. Hundreds of performers were given a chance to shine, and thousands of people were exposed to a fantastic genre of music they may not normally have mentioned.

The Soho Jazz Festival did exactly what I wanted it to – it brought people together in the borough of Soho, allowed them to have a great time and listen to a genre of music they may not have previously heard. It was a great success, and I was happy to see that the feel-good factor continued long after the Festival ended (which meant good news for the takings in PizzaExpress, which was by now synonymous with the London jazz scene).

Inevitably, by the time the Earth had spun around the sun another time, people were asking me about the 'Second Soho Jazz Festival', and it seamlessly became an annual event. I approached the artist Eduardo Paolozzi to create fantastic posters promoting the event. I had become close friends with Eduardo ever since his Spirit of Brunel lit up my Swindon PizzaExpress. He was a thicket, black-haired charming Italian man, with huge hands thickened from a lifetime of fashioning heavy sculptures.

Eduardo's posters were often collages of jazz instruments or even the musicians themselves, and they were always vibrant, eye-catching and instantly iconic. He was a true master of the trade. One memorable creation, in 1987, saw a poster which showed nine headshots, each of whom were made up of four-or-five of the performers' faces. It was a perfect depiction of the amalgamation of music we put on, all under one umbrella.

The festival ran for 16 magnificent years before coming to an end in 2002. I take great pleasure in the knowledge that the countless performances by talented musicians helped to spread the joy of jazz with thousands of people.

At the Festival with Gaston Berlemont, who ran The French Pub in Soho

33
BEFRIENDING A
DICTATOR'S SON

Of course, while I was running the Jazz Festival there was also the small matter of being in charge of PizzaExpress. Often, quirks of fate meant that the two overlapped.

For example, on one occasion in the late 1980s I travelled over to Forli, in the east of Italy, to sample new ingredients. My traveling partner was Dickie Bird, and the purpose of the trip was to taste a potential new supplier's tomatoes.

The trip started at Heathrow Airport. I have spoken of my dislike for the London Tube, but that pales in comparison to my disdain for airports. Flying should be the most wonderful spectacle – a truly great human achievement that has helped erode archaic feelings of national boundaries to create a truly globalised world. And, lest we forget, it sends you flying above the Earth's core at hundreds of miles per hour.

However, when you go to an airport all this sense of wonder is replaced with a very dull, insipid experience where you are asked to queue, queue and then queue again. I hate the places with a passion, and although I love to travel, I hate the process of flying.

Heathrow Airport was the usual disaster zone. The flight Dickie and I were booked on to was postponed for some reason, and the next flight wouldn't be until tomorrow. That was the date of our meeting with the tomato suppliers, so understandably we were disappointed.

However, the people around me were descending into madness. Men in suits were banging on desks like caged zoo animals.

It was amongst the chaos that I spotted a man who looked like a pilot, on account of some stripes on his jacket. I didn't know what the stripes meant, but from this small status symbol I assumed he was an important man. I calmly approached him, and must admit that I dropped the 'PizzaExpress founder' into my introduction, just in case he was a fan.

I explained how important it was that we get to Italy to taste these tomatoes, which could revolutionise the pizzas in the restaurants. If Dickie and I didn't get there, maybe we would lose the deal and thousands of restaurant goers would be denied the chance to taste the finest tomatoes in Italy.

The next thing I knew, we were summoned to the gate and told to sit in the executive lounge to catch a club class flight to Germany, then directly on to Italy. We would arrive 90 minutes late and in better seats than the ones we had paid for, for no extra costs. I suppose the man was a PizzaExpress fan after all.

It just goes to show, a little diplomacy sometimes goes a lot further than anger when things aren't going your way.

After we eventually got to Forli, the tomato trip was a bust – I didn't like the taste of their produce, and thought our current suppliers offered a better taste at a cheaper cost. A little disappointed at the anti-climactic trip, I insisted that we hire a car and go to Forte dei Marmi for a couple of days. It was a nice excuse to revisit my old teenage stomping ground.

On the drive over there, the radio station played a song by jazz musician Romano Mussolini, son of former

Italian dictator Benito. The wonderful, expressive music played on the radio was the polar opposite of the kind of systematic unity this man's father promoted when he ruled Italy for 21 years, before being usurped and eventually executed by his former subjects.

As we approached Forte dei Marmi, Dickie and I spoke of how perversely wonderful it was that a country that had murdered a leader were able to embrace his son as an artist. Upon finding a little hotel near the seaside, I practiced my Italian by asking the receptionist if she had heard of Romano Mussolini.

Amazingly, she replied by saying, "It's funny you should say that, because he is playing in the club over the road from here tonight." After dumping our bags in the room, we immediately went to the club, despite it being the middle of the day and presumably hours until the show started.

When we entered, we asked the barman what time Romano Mussolini would take to the stage. He pointed to a man drinking on his own and said, "Why don't you ask him yourself?".

Hearing this, Romano cackled and invited us over to sit with him. Dickie is not an Italian speaker, so we talked candidly in English like old friends for hours. In the course of one afternoon I had gone from learning of this infamous fascist's son being a talented musician, to befriending him over drinks! It was the fastest turnaround since those Greeks took their wooden horse to Troy.

Romano was around 60 years old at the time, and it did strike me that his father was roughly the same age when he died. However, the subject of his dad was never brought up – and why should it have been? I wouldn't expect him to talk about my father, and Dickie wouldn't have expected Mr Bird Sr to be mentioned.

I later learnt that he had performed under an assumed name until 1956, but had since formed the "Romano Mussolini All Stars", who were one of the country's leading jazz bands. He was also a jazz pianist and painter, and also dabbled as a film producer, but seemed less enthusiastic about that.

I explained that I had set up a Jazz Festival in Soho, and Romano was delighted to hear that an English person was trying to promote it in London. He said he would love to come and perform in the capital – and like a flash, I said that he could headline the next festival. Romano was delighted at this idea, and we shook on an agreement there and then.

We talked for about two hours, and then he had to go and prepare for the show. When we returned to the venue, a sofa had been placed in front of the audience at the edge of the stage. A barman told us that the seat was for us, and sure enough there was a sign reading *'Per Peter e Dickie… godersi lo spettacolo'* – 'for Peter and Dickie… enjoy the show'.

We sat in perfect view of what was a most fantastic performance. After the concert finished, I again warmly shook Romano's hand and swapped telephone numbers with him, again expressing my desire for him to come to London for the next Soho Jazz Festival.

On the flight back home, I started to get some reservations about it. I had thoroughly enjoyed Romano's company, his courtesy and most of all his performance. However, I was also aware how the headline of "Mussolini's son coming to festival" may be misconstrued.

I didn't want political nuts ruining the ambience of the festival by coming along and turning it into a protest.

But the more I thought about it, the less inclined I was to cancel the booking. Romano had proven himself to be a perfect gentleman, and to tar him with a brush because of the things his father was accountable for seemed totally unfair.

So I stuck with the booking, and I'm pleased to say that my fears were unfounded. There was no protest, Romano's visit came and passed with nothing but terrific warmth from the music-loving public, and it was a great success.

CHAPTER VII:
POST PIZZA AMBITIONS

After your pizza is fully cooked, it is taken out of the oven and handed by the pizzaiolo to the waiter to be served.

Just like every pizzaiolo has to hand over the dish he has lovingly created, every businessman has to know when their time is up. No job is permanent, and you have to be astute enough to realise when to hand over to another person.

At a ball with Suzie Elliott and my sister, Mary Clementine (aka 'Wendy')

34
THE END OF AN ERA

I have always thought my brain is geared more for creativity and entertainment than hard business and finances. Thankfully, I have been lucky to be surrounded by people who helped steer me in the right path in those regards – especially Ron Simson.

For much of the time PizzaExpress functioned, Ron advised me financially. But it was in 1992 that he decided he wanted to be out of the business.

Ron announced that 27 years was enough time to help his old university friend running PizzaExpress, and told me that he wanted to sell up and move on. This came as somewhat of a surprise to me, and made me start to consider my own position.

I was 63 years old – fast approaching retirement age and starting to think of the next stage of my life. However, I had no desire to retire to some beach in Barbados and sip on rum for the rest of my time on the planet. I still had a plethora of ambitions to fulfil – most pressingly, a desire to improve my hometown of Peterborough.

When I started to tumble towards the age that society dictates people stop working at, I started to think about what I would do when I was a 'pensioner'. Ron's decision to move on really accelerated that thought process. You only have a certain number of years on the planet – you need to make sure you do everything you wanted to do before you go.

Frankly, I didn't see the everyday running of PizzaExpress as one of my priorities. I felt I had achieved everything I possibly could with the restaurant.

My Christian faith told me that it would be best to spend my fortunes on helping other people – to invest my money in ways that it could benefit others. Nothing had given me greater pride than raising cash for the Venice in Peril Fund, and I thought the buzz of similar philanthropic projects could continue to inspire me well past the age of 65.

I also realised that PizzaExpress Ltd was only one of my business interests. Within Peter Boizot Franchise Ltd, I held Pizza on the Park and Kettner's, and I felt confident that these two fantastic restaurants would keep me busy and out of the poor house!

And so, with a heavy heart, I decided to move on from my role in charge of PizzaExpress. The franchisees and employees were saddened by my decision, and I was especially touched by Eddie Kidney's assertion that he had hoped I could carry on at the head of the company forever.

When I decided to join Ron in selling my stake in PizzaExpress Ltd, I was aided greatly by my nephew, Matthew Allen. He is, along with his sister Sarah, the closest thing I have ever had to a child of my own. Matthew lived with me for a time in the flat in Lowndes Square. Matthew had a law degree and qualified as an accountant, so it's safe to say he has brains for business.

He was also my family member, and therefore extremely trustworthy. All of this made me feel he would guide me along the right path when I sold up and moved on.

Matthew explained to me that I technically owed my own company a lot of money, because I had borrowed some money from PizzaExpress Ltd for the Peter Boizot Foundation Ltd businesses. 'Stealing from Peter to pay Peter', if you will.

As a result of me not paying it, PizzaExpress Ltd was in some quite serious financial difficulty itself. Midland Bank agreed with this opinion, and they were pretty unhappy with the state of the business. This bamboozled me – how could a busy and thriving restaurant with low overheads ever struggle for money?

Thankfully, there were still plenty of people who wanted to buy PizzaExpress Ltd, and Matthew brokered the sale on my behalf. He kept me informed every step of the way, and I am very grateful for the way he helped me during that difficult time. Although I am calm in the long-term, I do have a spikey short-term temper and fear that may have got in the way of those negotiations.

By 1993, Matthew presented two options for me. The first would see me sell it to a person I would rather not name for £18 million. The second was a more complicated deal that left me with a silent stake in the company – something that I preferred because I still felt it had the potential to expand.

That deal would see me sell the business for £15 million to a company called Star Computers PLC, which was controlled by two men named Luke Johnson and Hugh Osmond. It was essentially a shell company, and would be renamed 'PizzaExpress'.

Importantly, that deal would see me given 10 million shares (which, at 40 pence each, were worth £4 million). Johnson and Osmond also proposed to put existing franchisee David Page as chief executive and chairman, while I would be the ceremonial 'president' (a title with no decision making power, but still afforded a place on the board).

These caveats appealed to me, as I didn't like the idea of totally leaving PizzaExpress, and this deal felt more like stepping to one side and letting someone else steer the ship I had built.

Matthew also advised me that the 40 pence value of each share would go up substantially, so the £3 million I was foregoing in selling outright for £18 million was actually a rather lucrative investment. Those 10 million shares could be worth many, many millions of pounds if the business grew under the new management.

And so I decided to do the deal. I sold to Johnson and Osmond's Star Computers Plc, who quickly rebranded their company as PizzaExpress Ltd. They stayed true to their word of keeping me on as the ceremonial president, and I am still paid a healthy annual salary by the company.

After PizzaExpress went public, I organised to meet up with Dickie Bird at the Wardour Street pizzeria. It seemed a fitting place.

We sat down and shared a Margherita Pizza, which was thankfully still 'on the house', and I reminisced about the last three decades and how this little restaurant had grown into something that could be floated on the stock market.

It was remarkable how far the journey had twisted and turned since Anne Mathew had dared me to open an Italian restaurant back in the mid-1960s. After eating, we took a stroll across Soho Square and I must admit I started to get rather emotional. Dickie asked me if I was upset, but I was not – I just recognised that this was the end of the journey for my control of PizzaExpress.

Since then, the company has continued to expand, and now boasts in excess of 400 branches across the UK and Ireland. I knew that it would continue to grow – it was a fantastic restaurant and if they kept the right ingredients, there was no reason to doubt its continued success.

I think Dickie and others may have felt I might have had some resentment towards the way things had gone. As the sun set across the Square, Dickie asked me if I would change anything. The question was even easier to answer than when the chairman of the RAC had asked me, "What is a pizza?".

I looked Dickie in the eye and replied, "I don't regret a single thing."

And that was the truth. It still is. I had run the restaurant for (almost) three decades. It was far more successful than I could have ever dreamed, and it had become a household name. I had nothing but pride about my time at PizzaExpress.

As my nephew Matthew wisely predicted, the value of my shares was far greater than the £3 million I gave up by not selling the company outright. When the company floated on the stock market in February 1993, my 40 pence shares increased by 250 percent to £1 per share on the very first day of trading. In one fell swoop, my £4 million in shares became £10 million.

Within a year, the shares had shot up to such a high value that I thought it would make more sense to sell them and re-invest them in something new. When I cashed out, the value was just shy of £20 million, which combined with the £15 million I had received outright for the sale left my bank balance in a very healthy position.

By the time everything had gone through it was 1994, and I was just a few months away from turning 65: the dreaded 'retirement' age. But even with a bank balance of £35 million, it was never my intention to stop working.

As Dickie Bird's wife had once told me, I was married to my work. To me, retirement would be like taking a divorce. And that could never happen.

At the same time, I did not want to start up another dynasty. I'd enjoyed very much being the figurehead of PizzaExpress, but now was the time for another chapter in my life. And it was in the autumn of my years that I decided to switch the focus back onto how I had spent the spring of my life.

I decided to commit to my gut feeling that I could make a difference in my hometown, and chose to spend the fortune I had earned to improve Peterborough.

But before I left Soho behind, I wanted to leave a little present. I wanted to add my own weave to its tapestry, in addition to my pizzerias.

I wanted to leave something behind to promote the vibrancy and inclusiveness of Soho, and decided to spearhead a movement to bring a statue of the American jazz legend Duke Ellington to Cambridge Circus – the busy intersection of Shaftesbury Avenue and Kings Cross Road.

That way, cars could whiz by and their drivers remember the spirit of Ellington, which had inspired me so much during my formative years.

Ellington had an inexhaustible songbook and for me summed up everything that was great about the free spirit of that most sublime of genres. It was also fitting that he was a black man – I felt that would provide a sense of the unity of Soho, where people of all creeds and colours would stand side-by-side.

The piece was commissioned for the sculptor Nicholas Dimbleby to create. It is a shame that Dimbleby is often overshadowed by his brothers David and Jonathan, as his quality as a sculptor is outstanding.

It showed Ellington leaning on a piano, dressed in a fine suit with trademark bowtie. This was to be my gift to Soho, and no expense was spared. I commissioned the statue to be an eight-foot bronze statue that weighed nearly a ton, and cost £100,000.

It was not paid for totally by me – a whole group of us cobbled our pennies together. Amongst those who contributed were fellow jazz lovers John Prescott, Spike Milligan and Sir Johnny Dankworth.

The statue was put up to great public acclaim… but sadly, the powers-that-be were not so keen. Almost as soon as the statue went up, it was removed after objections from Westminster City Council. Apparently it did not have the appropriate planning permission.

It was relocated to Pizza On The Park, but I felt that bureaucratic interjection summed up how that the carefree and fun Soho I had loved and fought to protect had sadly been swallowed up by the bureaucracy of London.

Much like PizzaExpress, my time at Soho had come to an end. But I am always hungry for success – and a new chapter in Peterborough awaited.

35

THE MOZZARELLA MILLIONAIRE'S NEW NECKLACE

I had always retained a link to Peterborough, be it visiting friends, family and the cathedral, or supporting the football and hockey teams. Peterborough was always home, and I loved it. But in the time I had left it had expanded from being like a lovely market town to being somewhat of a grubby small city.

Each time I visited, Peterborough seemed quieter and quieter. Gone were the small boutique shops in the city centre, replaced by a monolithic shopping centre called Queensgate, which brimmed with the same faceless brands that you would find in any other city. There was no vibrancy in the city, no sense of a unique identity.

So I decided to invest in my hometown, in the hope that I could help restore it to the glories of my youth. My plan was to buy three or four prominent buildings in the city centre and turn them into hubs where people could go with their partners, friends or family.

My ambition was not just to make money for myself – I hoped this spark could re-ignite the city of Peterborough. The analogy of a city being like a wrist-watch helps to explain this. Mechanical watches use a balance wheel and spring which act together like a pendulum. The mass of the wheel and the elasticity of the spring help to power the watch, and then gears are in place to push the second, minute and hour hands around the clock face.

In London, the councils and government were the steady hands that regulated and gave the platform for others operate (like a balance wheel). The multitude of private businesses worked with them to forever push things forward (like the spring), and then the media helped to publicise what was happening (like the watch's hands).

In Peterborough, the city council was there to regulate things. *The Peterborough Evening Telegraph, Peterborough Herald and Post* and *Hereward Radio* could publicise. However, the problem was that the entrepreneurial spark just wasn't there. With no businesses acting like the spring to power the watch, the clock face remained static. I hoped that, by creating a handful of places to go in the city centre, the footfall would increase and more 'springs' would follow.

I knew a lot of things were about to change in my life, and I needed somebody to help me to organise things. Quite by chance, I happened to meet a magnificent lady named Rosemary Warne.

We were introduced by a mutual friend, the solicitor Vanessa Watson, at Pizza On The Park. I was immediately impressed by her friendly but authoritarian poise – and was not surprised to learn that she was formerly of the army and had served as a teacher.

However, most interesting to me was the fact that she had also worked as a charity administrator and events organiser.

If I was to create a template for somebody to help me during this period of transition, it would have been Rosemary. But thankfully, she was very real and I was very keen on employing her.

I offered her the especially created title of 'Administrator of the Peter Boizot Group' – and she accepted to release me of the day-to-day management that I found so tedious. Rosemary often teased me that I didn't really delegate anything, because it was not in my nature to be hands-off, but we were a good match and Rosemary would go on to be an unparalleled support during difficult times that were ahead.

The very first thing I did was put in a bid of a couple of million pounds to take over the Great Northern Hotel. The magnificent mid-19th century building is the first thing visitors see when they roll into Peterborough railway station.

It was a grand old building, but I thought it had fallen into a poor state inside. If it was spruced up, it could be something that my fellow Peterborians would be proud to represent the city.

From the age of 10 I had seen the great and good going into Great Northern. Not only was it the first sight that greeted visitors to the city, it was also the place to be seen. Two grandiose bars, function rooms fir for a royal wedding, a beautiful garden and of course dozens of bedrooms – any of which could pass as a honeymoon suite.

When I bought it, I couldn't believe how it had been treated since then. To say it had fallen from grace would be unfair – it had plummeted with more gusto than a Soho stripper's stockings during a stag do.

Far from being a luxurious hotel that would host AGMs, political fund-raisers or high-end business meetings, it was now a rather nondescript bar attached to some cheap bedrooms.

The walls outside were crumbling; the walls inside were bare. The Great Northern needed a total overhaul that would cost another couple of million pounds to make it right. But I was determined to do that, to retain it for future generations.

Despite the good work of the excellent Peterborough Civic Society, it had still not been given listed building status to protect it against development and without imminent intervention this once fabulous building could be turned into yet another car park.

Places like Leicester and Cambridge have many fine Victorian buildings, and I didn't want people to have to leave Peterborough to see some 19th century heritage. So it was important to match the £2 million purchase with £2 million of improvements to make it fit for purpose.

Although the architecture of any restaurant is important, it is even more integral to the success of a hotel. A hotel's building creates its atmosphere, and a good ambience is a magnet to potential customers. In a hotel, you aren't selling food. You are selling a place to be a surrogate, temporary home, and I hoped to turn the Great Northern into Peterborough's 'must visit' venue.

I decided I wanted it to be like Kettner's, with a room for a bar and a room for a restaurant. People coming for food and drink have different demands – so why not give them different rooms?

The bar was painted red, and the dining room painted white. A jukebox was put in the bar, so we could have jazz music playing in the restaurant. It had high barstools, sofas and counter service in the bar, and then sunken chairs, private tables and table service in the restaurant. The two rooms became independent entities operating under the same roof.

The bedrooms were also all given a complete overhaul – freshly painted, new (four poster) bed frames, new sheets; the whole works. I wanted them to have the best wood panels, and the top rooms had state-of-the-art, en-suite bathrooms.

I adorned the walls of the hotel with the huge collection of art I had amassed over the years. I was never a big visitor of auctions – I would be more inclined to make an offer of a painting I happened to notice while eating in a restaurant. After a little haggling, I would often leave with a full belly and a masterpiece under my arm.

However, soon after I bought the hotel and moved back to Peterborough, sadness was to come in 1995, when my mother passed away. She was an elderly lady, and it was her time, but that was still obviously a time of great sorrow for me.

Somewhat inevitably, I found a way to channel my emotions through my work. I decided to dedicate the garden at the hotel to my mother, and transformed some shoddy looking shrubs into a fabulous lawn with flowers that could rival anything at the Chelsea Flower

Show. I felt it celebrated my mother's natural beauty and everlasting spirit.

It also became home to the eight-foot tall statue of Duke Ellington originally commissioned for Soho Square. 'The Duke' was transported up to Peterborough and left in the garden, much to the surprise (and sadly disappointment) of its creator, Nicholas Dimbleby. He argued that Ellington had no link to Peterborough, and questioned why it should be moved 80 miles north of its previous home in London. The reason for the move was not for publicity or to promote the hotel – it was inspired by my hope that the Duke's inimitable style would inspire the people of Peterborough in the same way that his music had inspired me.

The one expense I did hold back on in the hotel was putting crystal basins into the ladies' toilets. I had wanted them to add that touch of quality, but my sister Wendy and our dear friend Sue Woodcock managed to talk me out of it – they were only the bogs, after all!

It rapidly became a place to be seen in Peterborough, and no more so than for my 65th birthday party in 1994. It was a good opportunity to show off my new investment, and party-goers were treated to an unforgettable banquet of a thousand oysters, smoked salmon and lobster.

Around 600 people turned up for the party, including the jazz legend George Melly (who came sporting a striped jacket, leopard-print tie, outrageously flamboyant hat and trademark eye-patch). Those who came up from London were treated to a free ride in a train I booked especially. During their trip up to Peterborough, a jazz band played in the carriages and they were all treated to wine and nibbles.

I was pleased to celebrate my birthday with such close friends after a rather tumultuous 12 months – and I wanted to do it in style.

When they arrived, a giant marquee lined with flowers and decorations galore adjoined the main building, and featured a five-star buffet. My beautiful old wine cellar was decked out as a champagne and oyster bar that many quipped reminded them of Kettner's. Of course, all the bars were complimentary and well used by the guests. As was the giant chocolate fountain which I had installed especially for the occasion!

The guest list read like a who's who of Peterborough – footballers, MPs and local businessmen. Even the local journalists were invited, and they in turn wrote a lovely piece about the party in the *Peterborough Evening Telegraph*. I asked for no presents from anybody who attended – after all, it was my chance to lavish a party on them, so I didn't want to spend the whole time ripping through wrapping paper and untying ribbons.

When I throw a party, I like to do it well. And I really do think that was one of the best I have ever thrown. Just imagine what my 100th birthday party will look like!

I hired a lady named Emma Burston to be the manager, and yet again I got very lucky – she was fantastic. I'm not sure if I've got a knack for hiring the right person or have just been very lucky in my appointments. Much like with Dickie Bird and Eddie Kidney, we quickly became friends outside of work, and went on numerous holidays together.

In total, I hired 47 staff – including chefs, waiters, bell-boys, accountants, receptionists and managers. And these weren't any run-of-the-mill people; they were of the highest quality (and were of course paid accordingly).

It was an expensive pursuit, but if this was going to be a prestige hotel, it wasn't going to come cheap. We had a fantastic team, and by the time we opened, I felt the hotel could rival the finest in London.

What was without doubt was that we were the best hotel in Peterborough, and as well as being a good place to stay for the night we marketed ourselves as somewhere for people to pop in for a drink or book a table for a meal.

I also decided to turn one of the hotel buildings into an exhibition of art, named the 'Guildenburgh Art Gallery'. It was free for people to visit. Although I was of course aware that this could increase footfall to my hotel (and more pertinently its bar), it also finally afforded me somewhere to publicly display my art collection. Hanging pride of place in the gallery were some fine jazz pictures by the inordinately talented Leo Meiersdorff.

My collection was over 800-items strong that was valued conservatively at £60,000. Of course, they had price tags and if people wanted to buy them that was welcomed, but this was a walk-through art gallery – the likes of which Peterborough had never before seen.

36
WORKING FROM HOME

I actually liked the hotel so much that I decided to become a permanent guest. I moved into one of the luxurious suites – I had already bought the four-poster beds after all, so I might as well sleep in one. It never felt like I was staying in a hotel. I suppose because I had put all my little touches to the place, it was more homely than any hotel I had ever stayed in before.

We even got two pets for the hotel – Moët and Chandon (named, of course, after the drinks). They were both white cats, as you would expect from their champagne-derived names, and were very friendly with the guests. They soon became popular attractions, especially Moët, who was a house cat and could often be found in the bar.

Chandon was a little bit more adventurous and would often nip into the train station opposite. One day she completely disappeared – I'm not sure if she had been misconceived as a stray or if she had been caught on a train and ended up in Edinburgh.

My dear friend Renée Brittain was staying at the time, and we went out looking all over Peterborough for Chandon and put up 'missing' signs, sadly all to no avail.

After a couple of weeks, I decided to go to a cat sanctuary in Wansford and get another cat of a similar appearance, who became the new 'Chandon'. We never told the guests that it was a different cat – although the hotel's newest arrival did have an obvious discrepancy from the original. Let's just say if you raised Chandon I's tail you would see a different sight to Chandon II's rear private parts!

Luckily, nobody ever noticed that Chandon had seemingly undergone a sex change, and he lived happily with his sister Moët for years to come.

People from all walks of life would drink in the bar and the cats were happy to play with them. I have since read of Parisian cafes were patrons can pay to play with one of a dozen resident kittens because of their therapeutic qualities. Apparently the place is fully booked out by French people looking for some moggy affection months in advance.

With hindsight, maybe I made a mistake giving Moët and Chandon's affection away for free – perhaps if Ron Simson or Dickie Bird were still advising me, he would have shown me a way to turn the idea into a profitable business!

While the cats projected a calming atmosphere, there is always a possibility for drama when alcohol is being served. One such occasion regrettably saw somebody use their camera phone to film a verbal altercation that took place in the bar. The clip ended up becoming something of a regrettable internet sensation.

The two-minute video saw a patron frustrated after service was refused because she was thought to be too drunk. It was posted onto YouTube and caught the attention of some of the national newspapers, and quickly became a major story.

I was disappointed to achieve that unwanted publicity, but not because of the actions of the customer – I was more disappointed with the bartender. I could not understand was how the situation had unravelled in the first place.

I watched the video, and the customer did not seem to be intoxicated beyond the point of reason. Although I agree that somebody who cannot reason rationally or stand on their own two feet must not be served alcohol, that didn't seem to be the case on this occasion. So why were we declining to serve her?

Bars are there to serve people alcohol – and I have been served many times while in a tipsy state. Who hasn't? A bar not serving people because they have already been drinking is like a restaurant not serving fat people.

The whole matter was a terrible shame and the absolute opposite of the sort of publicity we wanted for a high market establishment.

Sadly, the hotel was not a huge financial success, either in terms of attracting overnight guests or patrons visiting the bar. It was certainly not the roaring success I felt it deserved to be.

I was proud to have built the hotel to such a high quality and standard, but people complained to me that it sat opposite an ugly and noisy train station. I thought the location was great – it allowed commuters and tourists to step off the train, and come straight into the hotel. Sadly, it seemed like the sound of trains put guests off the hotel.

I'd envisioned the Great Northern bar as a place for young professionals in their 20s, 30s and 40s, with contemporary artwork and a saloon ready for raucous scenes. However, the people who trickled in tended to be older considerably older than that lucrative, desired demographic. They were in their 70s or above, and it never caught on with the younger audience.

I'm afraid to say the hotel started to lose a lot of money, and people quickly urged me to sell up and move the building onto somebody else. I had worked too hard for that, and had no intention to do so. Much like the Jersey PizzaExpress, I was sure that things would come good, and so I kept my faith in the hotel.

By 1994, *Jazz Express*, a magazine I had set up under the PizzaExpress umbrella, felt a little removed from me after I had sold my shares. I decided to set up a new glossy publication, which I rather cheekily named 'Boz', an eponymous title to reflect a magazine that was dictated by my personal tastes.

It was sold through WH Smith and to a loyal army of around 1,000 subscribers. The magazine was sold for £1.50 and each monthly edition was read by probably around 2,000 people – a thousand in the shops and the thousand who subscribed. It was a small venture, but one which I enjoyed very much.

It was unashamedly a magazine that put forward matters of interest to the Peter Boizot Group. It would be a portal of information about Kettner's, Pizza on the Park and the Great Northern Hotel in Peterborough.

But it was also a place for culture lovers to get their information. My star columnist was Larry Adler, who was a fantastic jazz musician. I first heard Larry in 1935, when my father proudly brought his record into our home. I was hooked straight away.

We carried adverts at very cheap rates and the idea was for it to be an alternative to *Time Out* magazine. The main difference was that any event I was promoting would get the front page splash in every edition!

I remember doing an interview with a reporter from *The Independent* and he was astounded that I hadn't done any market research into what people wanted to read. But it fell into line with the same principles I had with any business venture I embarked upon: if it does well, great. If it does badly, at least I would have fun.

The magazine cost £5,000 per issue to produce, yet we brought in little more than £3,000 through sales and advertising. So it was something that I ran at a loss. I wasn't too concerned with the profit margins, but it does disappoint me that the printed media seems to be dying a slow and painful death.

I wanted *Boz* to be a public sphere for like-minded people, but I suppose mobile telephones and the internet have meant correspondence is much more immediate these days. You can check online when you are bored and find out what is happening on the other side of town, then jump in a taxi and get there straight away.

I prefer the old-fashioned way, when you would organise in advance – that way you could make sure you found time for everyone. You made sure you saw your girlfriend, your friends and your family members. If you play it by ear, one or more of those groups could suffer.

I suppose I must be stuck in my ways, as I still organise my social life at the start of a month with an open diary and a glass of wine, rather than minute-by-minute as seems the contemporary way.

37
A RESTAURANT FOR MY FATHER

M y next step to improve Peterborough was to set up a restaurant and café in the heart of the city. I specifically wanted to create this restaurant on Broadway – the biggest road in the city centre.

Broadway was formerly a road surrounded by small businesses and quirky shops. However, since the opening of the nearby Queensgate Shopping Centre, it seemed as though the shops had migrated away and been replaced by tacky chicken takeaways and cheap bars.

As a result, footfall was down, which also affected the nearby outdoor market and Broadway's public library. It had got so bad that Broadway's old Odeon cinema, which had entertained Peterborough since 1937, had stood empty since 1991. Decreasing attendances and the cost of keeping such a grand building in business had caused lease holders from the Rank Organisation to pull the plug.

It seemed like the council had no desire to improve the situation on Broadway, so I thought I would try my best to improve the area myself. I hoped that somewhere with a bit more class could help rejuvenate that side of town.

I found an empty plot (which was not too difficult), made a successful bid, and decided I would name it Gaston's, the name of my father. He had helped to inspire me so much, even after death, and this felt like a fitting tribute to him.

The menu at Gaston's was extremely different to PizzaExpress' – much more varied, including a large amount of Thai food. This was because the demographics of people in Peterborough were incredibly varied, and I wanted the menu to reflect that. Of course, there was also a hearty amount of vegetarian food on offer.

I would describe both Gaston's as a moderate successes. It was not financially rewarding for me, but it was spiritually rewarding. Many people enjoyed the restaurant, and I was touched by the plaudits I received for my hopes to improve Peterborough.

Even Mark Wright, the man appointed as poet laureate for Peterborough by the city council, was critical of our town's culture. He said that "Peterborough is a law unto itself. I just think it's the way society has gone in Peterborough – it's in a quagmire."

I believe he had performed a rather sparsely attended recital in the library on the same road as the art gallery. I do wish that he had come to visit the Guildenburgh Art gallery, as it boasted a lovely selection of art work by famous names like Eduardo Paolozzi to complete unknowns.

I decided that although I could help somewhat by giving artists exposure in the gallery, what the grass roots arts scene really needed was a bit of money. This led me to try to recreate what I had done with my Venice fund-raising to bring in some money for the Peterborough Arts Trust.

And so, the Petriburgian Pizza was born. The name comes from the collective noun for past pupils of the Kings School, but I felt could be adopted by people from all over Peterborough. The pizza was topped with mozzarella cheese, asparagus, stilton, olives and tomato. It was sold at Gaston's and, like the Venice in Peril fund-raiser, saw 25 pence of every sale go to the Peterborough Arts Trust.

I hoped that thousands of pounds would be raised and presented to groups and individuals, such as concert organisers and music groups. The head of the Peterborough Arts Trust was Dr Jim Deboo, a wonderful servant to the city and as fine a gentleman as your will ever meet. He was delighted with the donation.

I would later go on to sell the 'Petriburgian Style Bubble and Squeak' at the Great Northern Hotel – also at a surcharge of 25 pence, and also greatly appreciated by Dr Deboo.

I was less appreciative with the actions of burglars who broke into Gaston's one night and took £1,400 worth of champagne. It seemed as if it was a bit of a 'Trojan Horse' approach to burglary; police believed the thieves could have posed as customers, and then hidden when the restaurant was locked up.

When police were called, the burglars had escaped with the champagne. However, they had also been into the art gallery and placed six of the paintings onto the floor. It seemed as if they had intentions to steal the art, but were disturbed before fleeing the scene of the crime.

Such actions are despicable, and I praise my Christian upbringing for helping me to overlook such incidents and retain my positive opinion of the human race.

Every cloud has a silver lining, and the theft of my champagne brought another business idea. When I was bemoaning the fact they had stolen "my champagne", it dawned on me that this wasn't really "my champagne" – it was champagne I had imported from somebody else.

Anybody who knows me will tell you that this realisation inevitably made me think, "Why haven't I got my own champagne", so that's exactly what I did next.

I launched my own champagne label, eponymously named 'Boizot'. The drink was sold in Gaston's to moderate success, and soon led me to expand again into the bottled water market. I ordered 100,000 bottles of spring water from Westwood Farm, Bretton Gate, Peterborough, with the idea of cashing in on my hometown celebrity by selling them in Peterborough.

The name of Peter Boizot's bottled water drink? 'Pierre Boizeau', of course!

Sadly, launching 'Pierre Boizeau' was not one of my most successful business decisions. The spring water was not a big seller. Although its name raised a few smiles and got a substantial amount of press interest, takeaway drinks were not my speciality.

They went against the concept of investing in entertainment venues as social hubs that had treated me well throughout my life. Thankfully, I was savvy enough to realise that it was not my forte and decided to call that venture off – sadly, 'Pierre Boizeau' never really got off the ground.

CHAPTER VIII:
MONEY HAS NO OWNERS

After the cooked pizza is handed to the waiter, it is cut into small pieces before being served to the diners.

The penultimate chapter of my life story similarly saw me divide my money into a plethora of worthy causes. Whereas so much had previously been held in PizzaExpress, now I could redistribute into numerous smaller, worthy projects.

38

"IF YOU ARE LOOKING FOR A WAY TO LOSE ALL YOUR MONEY, BUY A FOOTBALL CLUB"

Shaking hands with the charismatic Barry Fry

At the turn of 1997 I committed to yet another new ambition that was also out of my comfort zone – but one that I felt was absolutely necessary. I decided to buy (and indeed save) the ailing Peterborough United Football Club.

Although hockey was (and always will be) my number one sporting love, I was a lifelong fan of 'The Posh' and was devastated to see the club fall on hard times. We always seem to be in hard times, but this felt more bleak than usual.

Posh are a team who tend to flitter between the third and fourth tier of the (four tiered) professional football pyramid. Every so often, we pop our heads up into the second division, but like a fish gasping for breath above the surface, we never stayed that high for long.

Posh were in the third division, but sinking like a stone to the fourth. The biggest danger was that we could fall even further. Posh were bottom of the league, crowds were down and the club was broke. There was a very real worry that the club could go bust and drop out of the professional leagues and into the dreaded abyss known as 'The Conference' – the amateur leagues.

To continue the fish analogy, this fish would be burrowing under the depths of the ocean, potentially never to return.

However, not everyone was quite aware of the mess the Posh were truly in. I found out about it after my interest snowballed following an invitation to a fund-raiser for the Peterborough United youth team at the club's stadium, London Road.

There was a three-course dinner in one of the lounges, and we were seated on tables which included one member of the team's under-18s side. I was immediately struck by two things – how much these young men wanted the chance to play football for their hometown club, and what difficulties they faced in doing so. They were paid a pittance, the training facilities were inadequate and matriculation to the first team squad seemed to be an alien concept.

It seemed sad that Posh would bring in a proven journeyman from another club rather than take a chance on an exciting young local talent.

One of the directors was Alf Hand, who I had known from King's School (although Alf was a couple of years below me). I said to him that I wanted to help these young footballers' dreams come true and offered the club a donation of £5,000 for the youth set-up. However, I didn't have my cheque book with me, so I asked Alf to come and see me in the Great Northern Hotel for breakfast the next day, when I would hand it over to the club.

That next morning, it was not Alf who turned up for the cheque – it was Posh's charismatic manager, Barry Fry. He was an enormous personality in the game, who had come through as a player at Manchester United then managed Birmingham City before joining Peterborough. Barry had a fine footballing pedigree, and was also a man who I warmed to immediately. Barry is a barrel-chested, old-fashioned and no-nonsense chap, whose mind works at one-hundred-and-fifty miles per hour, and his mouth somehow keeps up.

He was incredibly grateful for the £5,000 donation, and said it was appreciated by everybody at Peterborough United Football Club. I asked him how much difference it would make, and he was quite honest in his answer – he said not very much difference. Barry then explained to me that the Posh were on the brink of financial disaster, and although the £5,000 was greatly appreciated, if I really wanted to make an impact I'd have to hand over £2 million.

This made me realise that a gargantuan challenge lay ahead for the Posh – and never to be one to shy away from a challenge, I thought I could be the one who turned around its financial hardships. I decided that I didn't want to just give a few thousand to the youth team – I wanted to take over the whole club as chairman.

I recognised that the club's London Road stadium was another building that could act as a conduit to Peterborough back to life. It had a capacity of 12,000 people, and if you get 12,000 people into the city centre, the knock-on effect of the increased footfall would be fantastic for other businesses.

I phoned my old cricketer friend Doug Insole CBE, who had a seat on the FA board and was an expert in all things football. Never one to mince words, Doug's words fired as straight as if shot from the barrel of a shotgun. "If you are looking for a way to lose all your money, buy yourself a football club."

Doug, and others, warned me that being a football chairman eats away at your money like an insatiable tapeworm. Once you have control of the club, everything is down to you. Despite their name, Posh had nothing – and I would have to take everything on. The players' wages, the coaches' wages, the electricity bills, the heating costs. In both the stadium and the training ground. If things go well, you get promoted. And then the fans want new, better players. With higher transfer fees, signing-on fees, agent costs.

Doug explained that it was impossible for a chairman to make money, and it was also impossible for him to be popular. Bournemouth had just declared debts of almost £4 million. He said that I would inherit identical problems if I took over the Posh, and the fans would want nothing but an endless tap of money from the local lad famous for being in the *Sunday Times'* Rich List.

Football fans crave success. Success brings promotion. Promotion brings struggle. Struggle brings relegation. Relegation brings unpopularity. It's a vicious circle.

Make no mistake about it – this was a way of losing money, and becoming unpopular. Some people think I was naïve when buying a football club – nothing could be further from the truth. I knew the cycle – I had been a football fan for years, and had seen the routine pass many times.

But I knew that if I didn't stump up the money or this club, it would go under. Children would be denied the experience I had going down with my dad and uncle to watch games at London Road. The aspiring trainees would never put on that Posh shirt and hear the roar of their hometown crowd.

I could not bear the thought of Posh becoming non-league, and drifting around the amateur divisions. Damn the finances – my mind was made up. If I wanted to help Peterborough, I had to save Peterborough United.

I invited Barry down to Kettner's for a 'friendly chat', but in reality to discuss the possibility of me taking over the club. When he arrived, I immediately told Barry of my intentions. His usually beetroot coloured face turned an even brighter shade of red, as he clinched his fists together and punched the air in joy. This was Posh's get-out-of-jail for free card!

But Barry is a good man and he didn't mince his words either – he once again re-iterated that Posh were in a total mess – on and off the pitch. The way he painted the picture, Posh's chances of long-term survival looked bleaker than a Chekhov play being performed on a grey winter's day. In Barnsley.

I explained to him how everybody had warned me off buying the club, but I had ignored them in the same way I ignored people back in 1965 who had advised me not to open a pizzeria in London.

However, I had one condition – I wanted to focus things on the club's youth. I knew the first team was in danger of relegation, but I wanted the priority to be on developing the under-18s team first and foremost. Then, in a few years, that would benefit the first team.

I told Barry that it would mean money would be invested on training and infrastructure rather than buying lots of players. This was quite ironic, as Barry had bought so many players that one of the jokes doing the rounds on the terraces was that he was trying to sort out the city's unemployment problems single-handedly.

But Barry is a sharp operator, and he could see the benefits of long-term investment over a short-term solution. With a typically exaggerated shrug of the shoulder, he bellowed, "Well it's your money Peter. You can spend it on what you like!"

I asked Barry to keep my intentions quiet – which he did – and invited him to celebrate the impending takeover approach by going for a drink in Soho. Always up for a good time, he agreed and when we walked into the street I started to realise there was more to this bubbly character than I first thought.

Every step of the way was a well-wisher putting their thumb up and greeting Barry like a long lost friend. After this happened half-a-dozen times in a minute, I asked Barry if he was a regular around Soho. He said he wasn't, but these people were 'football people', so they all know who he is. I had never seen a normal person so unaffected by having such fame.

Next we went into a pub to toast the future. As we clinked glasses and drank a couple of pints, an endless stream of people came to pat Barry on the back and say hello. He loved the attention and seemed totally at ease with the attention thrown onto him in the pub.

When we left, I looked Barry in the eye and asked, "Are there a lot of gays in football?" He seemed surprised at my question, and he shot back a curt, "Not that I know, Pete."

"That's surprising" I replied, "Everyone knew you in there – and it was Soho's biggest gay bar!"

Meetings were swiftly arranged with Posh's current owners, who were only to keen to sell. My lawyers thoroughly checked the club's balances, and warned me that the situation was as bad as Barry had suggested. But my offer to take over the club was accepted so quickly it showed just how desperate the owners were to get out – a clear warning of the dangerous situation I was about to get myself into.

39
RUMOURS, RELEGATION
AND THE RADIO

Posh's London Road stadium

I won't go too much into Peterborough United's history on the pitch while I was chairman – anyone with the inclination to do so can read up the historical results in one of the Rothmans football annuals. But people don't know about what happened off the pitch – least of all that I was spending £1 million per year of my own personal money to stabilise the club.

So I'd like to lift the curtain to show you all the mad things that happen behind the scenes when you own a football club.

I owned 97 percent of the club, with around 200 shareholders owning the other 3 percent. I wanted the club to be for the people of Peterborough, so was glad for their involvement. It seemed nice that fans could buy in as shareholders for minor ownership for symbolic reasons, and also so they could take part in AGMs.

My main ambition was to create a team that would entertain people. Although league football was needed to bring in crowds, so too did good matches. It therefore came as a total surprise to me when reports in the national and local newspapers alleged that if my takeover was successful that I planned to replace the hugely entertaining and eccentric Barry with John Beck – a former manager of our rivals Cambridge United. Beck had a reputation for playing such attritional football that some of his former players allegedly demanded moves away.

I had no inclination to remove Barry as manager of the club – he had my full support and I planned to back him just like I had backed the managers of the PizzaExpress branches. As seems to be the case in sport, Barry is a positive character and told me that he wanted to not only keep Posh in this league, but take them up to the next one. I told Barry that I admired his ambition, but repeated that mine was not necessarily to rise through the divisions but just to play the best football possible.

He thought I was mad!

Here was a man who had dedicated the last 37 years of his life to getting results as both a footballer and then manager. Now his new boss was telling him to focus more on pizzazz than points!

However, I wasn't taking my position lightly and soon after taking over decided to invest £750,000 per year into the club's academy, and I put the youth team's highly-rated coach Kit Carson on a 10-year contract. Barry expressed some surprise that the youth budget was more than the first team budget – but it was the young players that attracted me in the first place.

I felt Kit's 10-year contract would provide continuity which would help him to create a dynasty that would give young men a chance of living their dream as a professional footballer. The money went into new training pitches and also educating these young footballers, so even if they didn't get on with an athletic career they would have something to fall back on.

The issue continued after my first match as chairman. We were away at fellow relegation strugglers Shrewsbury Town, and I took the coach with the players up to their stadium, Gay Meadow. Before the game, Barry told me that the two teams almost always drew. The last five games had been ties, and they had alternated to a perfect sequence of being 1-1 then 2-2, another 1-1 then a 2-2, and then another 1-1. I joked to Barry that this game was fated to end 2-2.

As I took my seat in the directors' box, I regained that youthful excitement about the start of a football match – this was a feeling I was desperate for thousands of people from Peterborough to continue to experience for years to come. That first sight of a freshly-cut football pitch is always something that takes my breath away.

Of course, I let Barry pick the team and spoke not a word to him or the squad during the game. It was a pulsating match that saw momentum shift to each team, but we soon went 1-0 down to a scuffed opening goal. My heart sank, and I must admit that a thought crossed my mind while I sat in the freezing cold Gay Meadow that maybe my 'retirement years' could be better spent on a beach in Barbados, surrounded by my millions. But I'm not wired that way – and if I was, I wouldn't have been rich enough to own a football club anyway.

Soon enough, I was shaken from my daydream by a fantastic, wonderful, scrappy equaliser by our ageing winger Louie Donowa, a loan player past his modest best at 32 years old. But after getting us the equaliser, he was my new favourite player!

Minutes later, we sensationally took the lead when our central midfielder (and now policeman) Scotty Houghton made it 2-1. However, we came crashing back down to Earth with a bang when Shrewsbury grabbed a late (undeserved) equaliser. So, as fate would have it, it was a sixth successive draw and the results sequence was still intact.

I was a little disappointed with getting one point for the draw rather than all three for the win, but I was happy with the way the match had gone. I decided that I wanted to let the players know this. So, after the final whistle, I jogged onto the pitch and called the players and Barry over for an impromptu team-talk.

As we huddled at the halfway line, I told them "I am not bothered if we win, lose or draw – if we have enjoyable matches like that every week, I'll be happy". Little did I know, but there was a roving cameraman on us at the time and my words were broadcast to the whole country.

Bear in mind that this is a sport described by the great Bill Shankly as being more important than life and death. He said it as a joke, but it was a stance commonly held by many fans on the terraces. And so, the first criticisms came.

I listened to a local BBC radio football phone-in, and the fans were already suspicious about me. They said they wanted a man who would lambaste the players for giving away a 2-1 lead – they thought I would be seen as a soft touch, somebody who the footballers would not be afraid of. Once the first criticisms came, so did others.

Questions over why, if I didn't care about success, I hadn't bought the club years earlier. There was even a conspiracy theory that I would sell the stadium and move us out of Peterborough – bonkers, and totally lacking in any semblance of truth.

The honeymoon was over, before it had even begun. Thankfully, I loved the club and its fans, even if it would feel as if they didn't really love me back.

My first half-season ended disappointingly when we, as expected, were relegated from the third to the fourth tier of English football. The inevitable eventually happened at home to Luton Town, after we lost in a do-or-die game bathed in the spring sunshine at London Road. In football, there are always rumours that managers are about to get sacked, and I think Barry thought he was walking the long mile to the chairman's office when I called him to join me in my office after the match.

But, just like I was not in the business of closing restaurants, I was not in the business of making my staff unemployed. I told Barry that all was not lost. The club was now on solid footing, and I backed him to bring us back up with exciting young players.

Sadly, my enthusiasm for the club's bright future was misinterpreted by the club's fans. I went onto Radio Cambridgeshire and, after an irate caller said I had failed to financially support the club. I explained how much work had to take place off the pitch before the team got better.

I explained how we had great young players coming through now, such as our teenage wingers Matt

Etherington and Simon Davies. But the fan said I had ruined the next year of his life because the club had been relegated. My response would haunt me for the rest of my time as a chairman. I uttered the infamous words, "You shouldn't take it so seriously. It's only a game."

It would be shouted at me for years afterwards by the fans whose club I had helped save. The reaction to this statement was nothing short of apocalyptic. It was plastered on the back page of the newspapers and even made national news. This, despite the fact, of course, that football is a game.

Of course I realised that sport and its cultural impact are important – I had pledged to spend £1 million per year on the club, after all. But in the great scheme of things, it isn't going to ruin somebody's life if their football club gets relegated.

In the next two seasons, we toiled in the fourth tier finishing 9th for two successive seasons. It seemed like we would win as often as we would lose, but most importantly we played exciting football. However, the most constant variable was the staggering amount of money I lost financing the club every year.

A lot of my personal money went to the first team as well as the youth side, and we had players with Premiership experience like the striker Andy Clarke and midfielder David Oldfield with top-level wages.

But most exciting for me were the young players coming through the club's ranks, and none more so than the terrific teens Etherington and Davies. Etherington was a lightning-quick winger who made his debut when he was just 15 years and 262 days old. At that time he was a King's School pupil, so he was an obvious golden boy to me as a former schoolboy there myself. Davies was a cultured midfield player who Barry praised as possessing as fine a footballing brain as he had ever seen.

I would leave Barry to all things football related – he was the athlete and I was the businessman supporting him. In my fourth season as chairman, Barry had cobbled together a real first-rate side in the fourth tier. Etherington and Davies were sparkling in the team (as well as playing for the England and Wales under-21 sides respectively), and started to attract a lot of attention from top tier football clubs.

I received a phone call from one of Tottenham Hotspur's senior management team (whom I shall not name) asking me about bringing them to White Hart Lane. Now, as much as I loved watching these teenagers playing for Posh, I knew the chance to join Spurs was a great opportunity. I said I felt it would be immoral for me to selfishly block any move.

The Spurs representative said he was pleased with my stance, but claimed that Barry was asking for too much money for the pair. He put a piece of paper under my nose saying I would sell Etherington for £750,000 and Davies for £500,000 – a combined £1.25 million. I thought it was a shame to be losing them, but signed the paper to allow them to move on to the Premier League.

I told Barry about the deal that evening, and he was furious. Not because the deal had been made to sell them, but rather because of the specifics of the contract I had signed.

Barry explained to me that he had done a deal with Spurs that would see Davies go for £1.5 million and Etherington for £1 million. It soon became apparent that their representative had swindled me out of 50 percent of the transfer fee. An agreed price of £2.5 million had dropped to £1.25 million after I was subjected to the guilt of not allowing players to fulfil their dreams.

Thankfully, the players had not yet signed their deals, so Barry quickly put the brakes on the deal and told Spurs that we had caught wind of their cheeky tactics. This whole situation showed how I am not really a football man, and why I was so reliant on Barry being there to stop my good nature being taken advantage of by slick, immoral dealings.

Barry said he never wanted to do a deal with Spurs again, but I was adamant that Etherington and Davies should not be denied their big break. In the end, Spurs came up with a new offer that stuck to £1.75 million up front, but included numerous add-ons including a 15 percent cut of any future sales.

I'm delighted to say both went on to have fabulous careers and spent over a decade in the top flight of English football. Davies gained 58 caps for Wales, and Etherington went on to play in two FA Cup Finals. In the end, the add-ons Barry negotiated meant their transfers were worth £4 million – so he helped me dodge that expensive bullet.

But this story shows how much I relied on Barry's savvy know-how to survive in the snake-pit that is professional football.

40
SPONSORSHIPS AND SPICE GIRLS

I thoroughly enjoyed the cut-throat nature of running a football club. The fans were the most important thing for me, and I used to put great effort into personally writing my humorous programme notes for the fans to read at every home game.

I once welcomed "the redoubtable warriors of Hartlepool" to the club – this was not meant as a tongue-in-cheek bash at the away team, but just a way of spicing up the fixture for our supporters.

I used to love interacting with the fans. As chairman, I would have an unlimited number of tickets for the directors' box at home games, and was always keen to spread the wealth. Often, en route to the game from the hotel, I would walk into the bar and grab some people wearing football shirts and ask them if they wanted to be my guests.

They had expected to be in the terrace, but ended up sipping champagne with the directors. I loved bringing half-a-dozen people in for a surprise match day treat – and to a man, the lucky recipients would always be overwhelmingly thankful for the invitation.

One thing about the fans that perturbed me was the hooligan element. It was not as rife at Posh as with some other clubs, but there was an element of self-proclaimed 'hardcore fans' that would like nothing better than taking a train to Cardiff or Leicester and smashing their city centre up.

I always felt Posh were representatives of Peterborough when we went to an away game, and these fans were doing the city a great dis-service with their drunk and rowdy behaviour. I rarely went to away games, but I would see the fans coming back on the train in a drunken state on a weekly basis.

With the train station directly opposite the Great Northern Hotel, on one occasion I saw a gaggle of coarse hooligans piling out into the street, spitting and shouting in an unacceptably loutish manner. I was disgusted by this sight, and so went out to confront them.

However, I have always favoured the 'carrot' to the 'stick', and instead of berating them I invited them into the hotel bar to discuss things over a complimentary drink. They were happy to oblige – I think the free pint swayed it! When we sat down, I explained that the way they were behaving was not what I expected when I bought the football club. They were very reasonable and appreciated my sentiment, and I'm glad to say I never saw those fans causing any trouble again.

I think morality had a key role to play in all my business dealings, and no more so than at the football club. Money and cash-flows were always a concern at Posh, but I always wanted to promote a good, wholesome football club rather than get caught up in the endless pursuit of money. Something that summed this up perfectly was our sponsorship deals.

During one board meeting, a director announced that he had found a company who were prepared to pay £125,000 per season to splash their logo across the Posh shirt. Everyone grinned and clapped at the prospect of the deal – everyone, that is, apart from me.

I slammed my fist on the table and said, "I don't want a company on the front of the shirt – the only reason I bought Posh was to promote Peterborough United! So why put another company's name on the kit?"

The other directors pleaded with me – they said they could bring in a couple of decent players if we just put some corporate logo on the shirt. They reasoned that the kit would still have the Peterborough United badge, but it was no use. I would not sell out my vision of what the sacred Posh shirt should look like for the sake of making some fast money.

This bemused the other directors, but I was the chairman and had the final say on all matters. I concluded the discussion with a saying that Barry has reminded me of numerous times since – "I am not in business to make money". And so, for the next three seasons the club played in blue shirts with 'The Posh' written on the front instead of a lucrative endorsement deal.

In fact, I was so keen on promoting Posh rather than other companies that I actually brokered a deal where we would sponsor the Royal Academy of Arts in London for a whole exhibition, which would last from 22 January to 13 April 1998.

The deal cost us £250,000 and the players and fans were cynical, but I thought it was a great deal. Not only would it raise the club's profile, but it would help a much-loved national treasure. The exhibition was called 'The Art Treasures of England; The Regional Collections', and boasted 400 works of art from a hundred museums. As well as the country's best unknown regional artists, there were also masterpieces by Michaelangelo, Monet and Leonardo.

I thought it would be a smash hit.

I worked with the Academy to put on a bash to mark our sponsorship of the exhibition. All the players came along in full suits, and it was quite the sight to watch working-class footballers from the lower professional leagues hob-knobbing with some of London's cultural elite. But the boys loved it – none more than Barry Fry, who visited it six times during the four-month run.

Watching the players play keepy uppy outside the Royal Academy of Arts

But it doesn't take an accountant to realise that turning down a £125,000 shirt sponsorship, and then paying off £250,000 to sponsor something ourselves did not add up financially. That was indicative of how the club was being run – I was simply investing too much of my own money.

I gave an honest interview to the *Peterborough Evening Telegraph* in which I admitted I was personally spending a small fortune on the club – around £1 million per year. That was not going to cripple me immediately, but I did concede that I couldn't continue to lose such an amount for the rest of my life.

One totally unexpected threat to my finances came from the pop star Victoria Beckham, then better known as the Spice Girl 'Posh'. She obviously shared her name with my football club, although the team's history and heritage dated back considerably further. However, it seemed that the pop star going by the name of 'Posh Spice' had an issue with the club sharing the nickname, and was keen to ban us from using the word in commercial activities!

This was unfathomable – we far outdated her nickname – and also impossible to even consider. The nickname 'Posh' was loved by our fans. It appeared on all our shirts and souvenirs – white seats even spelt the word across the backdrop of blue seats in our main stand.

It seemed laughable to me, how could this long-standing trademark of the city of Peterborough be challenged by a pop star (albeit one married to the England football captain, David Beckham) who thought it was synonymous with her. This is the statement sent to the club by her representatives on the matter:

> *"The name Posh is inexorably associated with Victoria Beckham in the public's mind. The concern from her team is that they (the public) would think she had in some way endorsed products she had no knowledge of."*

We argued that we had a pre-existing trademark of the name, and although she may be recognised as *'Posh'*, there is no doubt amongst football fans that Peterborough United are, and always have been, *'Posh'*. If a Spice Girl had been called 'Villain Spice', would Aston Villa have been asked to change their name?

We didn't want her to stop using the nickname, but at the same time, we were stunned to receive the letter. Frankly, it would have been humorous if it wasn't such an attack on the club's culture and heritage.

We were inundated with messages of support from all over the country, including a rather humorous poem by Peterborough's poet laureate, Mark Wright. The same man who had called Peterborough 'a quagmire' came out in full support of the club with a humorous poem about the Victoria Beckham situation. It read;

Oh Posh Spice, you're really not so nice.
What makes you think you can take our name
And wear it with pride and shame.
You're like a common bird
As with all megalomania satisfaction
The Beckhams' Manchester United
catchphrase reactions.
You're not Posh – what tosh
A dead ringer for a barrel load of monkeys
Going greener by the day
You think Victoria you own the world
– But darling you're no debutante
Well not in my football play.
There is only one Posh
And they by the River Nene are boss,
You're just some loose change

> *Over crass glib debris that floated our way,*
> *Port out starboard home*
> *Abbreviated is our Rome*
> *So petty Victoria go home.*

After all the furore died down, so too did the trademark claim. Thankfully, the challenge was seen off and Posh continued to trade as a football club and Posh Spice continued to be a successful singer and fashion designer. As far as I know, nobody turned up to her gigs expecting to watch Peterborough United, and nobody came to London Road expecting to see a Spice Girl concert.

Perhaps the best thing linked to running a football club was the fact that anything and everything can happen. There were also humorous anecdotes to tell on the pitch as well as off it.

One time I settled down to watch us play away on the first game of a new season with Mark Plummer, a sports reporter from the *Peterborough Evening Telegraph*. When the players took to the pitch, I was shocked. Posh had always worn plain blue shirts, yet I was greeted by the sight of footballers sporting a garish blue-and-white hooped kit.

I flew into a trademark rage. "Who the hell decided we should wear hoops? It certainly wasn't me. Why didn't they pass it by me? They should be sacked!"

I couldn't be interrupted and, if I had my way, I was ready to haul the players off the pitch and forfeit the match rather than play in such a shirt. Then Mark grabbed me by the shoulder and calmly whispered in my ear, "Peter, that's the Reading team."

I had forgotten that Reading wore blue-and-white… so we had been forced to wear our away kit! We all had a good laugh about it – and it was far from my only kit-related confusion.

Another time I took an impromptu taxi to Greater Manchester to watch us play Oldham. It was a spur-of-the-moment decision, so I didn't read any previews ahead of the match and only got to my seat just after the game started.

The game was a one-sided stroll for the boys in blue, who blew the opposition away 2-0. After the game I gave Barry a warm congratulatory hug, but my manager replied with a shocked look. He explained that we were actually the team wearing *white*, as our kit clashed with Oldham's blue home strip.

Little did I know, but I had accidentally been cheering on Oldham as they cruised to a 2-0 win against my team!

As you can probably tell, although I enjoy football, I don't follow it as fanatically as many others do. I'd struggle to pick even the most famous players out from a crowd. For example, after a friendly match with Tottenham Hotspur in the late 1990s, I told their youthful looking man-of-the-match that if he tried hard, he could forge a successful career in football.

Afterwards, I was told that the player I thought was an aspiring trainee was actually Sol Campbell – an already established England international.

I remember such incidents warmly. I think other football chairmen take themselves a little bit too seriously. Football is supposed to be a fun, social occasion. After the success of our Royal Academy of Arts sponsorship deal, I wrote to all 91 other league chairmen and asked if they were each interested in putting in a couple of thousand pounds each and we could jointly sponsor another display.

I thought it would be a great way of putting something back to the community.

However, 90 of the 91 league chairmen totally ignored the letter. I only received one response, from Chelsea's Ken Bates. He praised me for my idea, but told me in no uncertain terms that if he had a couple of thousand pounds spare, he would be investing it into Chelsea Football Club – not an art gallery.

That isn't to say I scrimped on giving money to my club. I felt our unofficial clubhouse 'The 74 Club' looked a little bit ropey, and decided to give it a spring clean. But I didn't just put a shine on it – I gave it a full makeover.

I spent £80,000 on it, including Italian marble on the bar and a huge coat of arms. The club was renamed the David Seaman Suite, and still offers a grandiose place for fans to gather before and after matches.

I also invested on the pitch. Although I favoured giving youngsters a chance, I also brought in some experienced players. Howard Forinton was a 24 year-old striker who played for Barry's old club, Birmingham City. Barry was insistent that we bring him in for a quarter of a million pounds, although he had never really set the world on fire.

But I agreed to the deal, and brought Forinton in for £10,000 up front and the additional £240,000 spread out with £10,000 payments per month for the next two years. Sadly, everything in football is a gamble, and this one didn't really work out. He spent three injury-plagued seasons at the club and scored a modest 10 goals in 60 games, before being released on a free transfer.

When you add in a signing-on fee plus three years of wages, with zero transfer fee recouped at the end of it all, you see how so many football clubs are facing financial troubles.

But I held no grudges and got on well with the players, who I think get a bad reputation for their off-field pursuits. They were very keen to help promote Posh in the community, and were genuinely committed to making the most out of their careers.

That's not to say we didn't have our fair share of off-field incidents. One that sticks in the mind was after the Christmas Party in 1999. After a dignified meal in the Bull Hotel in the city centre, some of the players went on to a charity disco that was taking place in Sam Jones Gym. They apparently gate-crashed without paying the £3 admission charge, slid across a dance floor and tried to gain access to the female toilets. One player was even separated from a spat with a member of the public that left both parties bloody and bruised.

The event turned out to be a *Peterborough Evening Telegraph* Toys and Tins Appeal – so you can imagine what the headlines looked like in the next day's newspaper.

It was all excruciatingly embarrassing, and I told the squad to write a letter of apology to the gym. Although they were genuinely good apples, I think alcohol can lead the holiest of angels down the devil's path. To act foolishly is bad itself, but for these young men to fail to pay a £3 charity entrance fee was totally unacceptable – especially considering the small fortune I was paying them all in wages.

Thankfully, they all apologised very sincerely and the matter went no further. These young men were in the public spotlight, and one of the very few burdens of being a professional footballer is that you are a role model – you have to set a good example to the fans that pay your wages.

41
A VERY POSH PROMOTION

Luckily, Barry was making things good on the pitch. After toiling away in the dreaded fourth tier for three years that felt like an eternity, he steered us into the top six in the 1999-2000 season. That meant we qualified for the sudden-death tournament to see who would win promotion to the third tier – the play-offs.

We won four of our last six games of the season, and had lost just once in nine games. Now to get promoted, we had to beat Barnet in the two-legged play-off semi-final and then fight for a place in the higher division in a one-off knockout match at Wembley.

I was incredibly confident going into the Barnet game, and made a rare away-day trip to north London to watch the game. I travelled down on the team bus and told the players they were too strong for our amber-and-black rivals, and so it proved – our good form continued with a thrilling 2-1 away win.

The return leg saw a carnival atmosphere at London Road, and we secured our place in the play-off final with a comprehensive 3-0 victory, thanks to a hat-trick by inspirational captain David Farrell. That meant we won 5-1 on aggregate, and more importantly, sealed our place in the promotion final at Wembley.

Posh's opponents in that all-important promotion decider were Darlington. Again, I sat on the coach down to London with the players, and again tried to lift their spirits ahead of the big match. The final was on May 26, 2000, but the weather made it look like it was late autumn. The wind howled and the rain lashed down as we took our seats in the stand of the grand old stadium, which was due to be knocked down just months later.

Wembley was due for a total redesign, and this would be one of the last games ever played under its iconic Twin Towers. Tens of thousands of Posh fans were in the stadium – this was exactly what I wanted when I signed up to run the club.

The game was more nervous than that 3-0 semi-final win over Barnet. We were better than Darlington, but our northern rivals stubbornly defended wave after wave of Posh attacks. As the clock ticked down, I realised there were now just 15 minutes left. If one of our players slipped on the wet turf and Darlington sneaked in to score, we would be denied what I felt to be a just promotion.

However, with darkness falling and 75 minutes on the clock, a breakthrough came. A ball bobbled over the top of that previously impenetrable Darlington defence, and suddenly our star centre-forward Andy Clarke (signed from Premiership Wimbledon) was through on goal. He steadied himself, put his head up and… tapped it straight at the goalkeeper! I was paying this boy a small fortune every week, and he had blown our big chance.

Or so I thought.

The keeper could only push the ball away, and Clarke was first to react. This time there was no time to think, and Clarke relied on his top-flight instincts to lash the ball into the goal. The fans went wild… Barry went wild… I went wild! The next 15 minutes were a complete blur, probably repressed to avoid a nervous breakdown. But somehow we hung on, and with the 1-0 win claimed an unforgettable promotion.

After the final whistle, the players went up to collect the trophy from the royal box. Barry rushed over to my seat, gave me a big hug and an ever bigger kiss on the face. "You're coming on the pitch!", he ordered. I declined, and said it was the team's moment. The next thing I knew, he grabbed me and dragged me onto the pitch!

So there I was, on the Wembley turf where England won the World Cup in 1966, watching the Peterborough United players collect the play-off trophy in 2000. I was overcome by the emotion of it, especially the rapturous applause and cheers the Posh fans gave to me.

In all the excitement, Barry handed me the coveted trophy and told me to celebrate with it. And so, that's exactly what I did – I went on an impromptu lap of honour. In a merry jig that belied my 70 years of age, I went on a joyful lap of honour of the Wembley pitch holding the trophy aloft in the pouring rain. What a memory!

However, I have slightly more hazy memories of the celebrations that night. I organised a private celebration (also known as a lock-in) at the Great Northern Hotel, where one of the great untold stories of my time as Posh owner took place. The players all went out into town to drink and mix with girls, while all of the 'adults' (management and directors) came to the hotel bar.

After a few hours of eating and drinking, it was time for the toasts. I stood first, and praised Barry's management and all the hard work done off the pitch to get us promoted. Barry stood and thanked me and his coaches, and so on. It was all very warm and jubilant. However, that all changed after what I now see to be a miscommunication. Our highly regarded youth coach, Kit Carson, stood and gave a speech that praised everyone at

Posh, but had a light-hearted dig at Barry for not picking enough of his brilliant teenage trainees for the first team.

Barry replied, in usually colourful form, by telling Kit that he is the manager and he will pick who he jolly well wants. What had started as light banter soon became a quite colourful exchange. Kit claimed he had players who were as good as our previous youth team stars Etherington and Davies, but they were being denied their rightful place in the senior team. Barry was adamant that his decision to ignore them had been validated by winning promotion.

In the end, I decided to interject. I turned to Barry and said he knew my stance was always about putting youth first and results second, and if Kit thought the players were good enough, they should be given a chance.

A combination of constructive criticism after winning promotion and the alcohol that was flowing had caused the situation to get out of hand. Barry was furious at this perceived power struggle, and wasn't sure who to be more angry at – his chairman or the youth team manager.

I could see Barry was out of control and I told him that maybe it was time for him to go. This turned out to be a poor choice of words!

I meant it's time for him to go home, but Barry thought I meant it was time for him to permanently go away from the football club. Barry stormed out, thinking he had been fired by the man who stuck by him in relegation on the day he secured promotion! I let the situation simmer down and called Barry in the morning. He was still incandescent with rage, but I explained that it was never my intention for him to leave the football club.

Barry was my manager, and I never had any desire to change that. The misunderstanding was quickly resolved, and thankfully Barry continued as the boss. The management and players had impressed me so much that I decided to pay for us all to go on an all-expenses paid end-of-season holiday to Majorca. It was a fitting ending to a fantastic season.

CHAPTER IX:
NO REGRETS

After the food has been served, the oven is turned off. The pizzaiolo's job is done – but he can still take satisfaction from the enjoyment others get from his work.

In a businessman's life, losing power over the companies is analogous to the food being served. However, if the businesses were good, the entrepreneur can take solace from the fact they gave joy to so many people – and can continue to do so.

That is the true legacy of a good businessman.

42
THE FINAL JEWEL BECOMES THE FINAL STRAW

In 1998, the Sunday Times Rich List stated that I was the joint 428th richest person in the country, with assets worth £50 million. I never paid much attention to these lists, which seemed to fluctuate more than the waistline of a person equally addicted to PizzaExpress and Slimming World.

However, I was also not terribly interested with my worth. I knew that my bank balance was considerably less than the £35 million I had in 1993, but with so much tied up in assets with ever-changing values, I didn't know how much I was worth. So where is the value in comparing a wild guess about my wealth with a wild guess about somebody else's wealth?

Doug Insole loves telling a story of the time when we were at an England football game at Wembley also attended by then-chairman of Tottenham Hotspur (and current star of *The Apprentice*) Sir Alan Sugar – who was listed at number 429 on the list. In good humour, I walked up to Sir Alan, offered my hand and said, "Hello number 429. I am number 428."

I thought this would be a light-hearted introduction, but he didn't like it much. His reaction was to coldly look me in the eye and then walk away without replying, which suggested to me that he cared a lot more than me about that rather silly newspaper list.

The Sunday Times' article again stated that I was losing £1 million per year on the football club. The word 'lose' was regrettable – that money was not 'lost' – it was invested into a business that would improve, lead to higher attendances and more footfall for my own restaurant, gallery and hotel in the city centre.

As much as I loved running these businesses, there was one last item I wanted to add to the necklace of my Peterborough empire – a spectacular arts complex that could host music, theatre and comedy performances.

I had loved seeing the shows in London, and very much thought that bringing a similar vibe to Peterborough would get my city up and running. I had been encouraged by the progress made at my other venues, even though none of them were turning a profit. But it felt like they were creating an attitude shift in Peterborough – and I felt with this one last push, my hometown could really kick on into being a 21st century city.

What I didn't know was that this 'final piece in the jigsaw' would prove to be the final strain on my resources.

I thought the one thing that would really aid Peterborough more than anything else was an all-singing, all-dancing arts venue. Somewhere that could house the top names in music, theatre and comedy.

Since 1991, the old Odeon cinema complex next door to Gaston's had remained dormant. The building was old and falling apart, but with a lick of paint it would be perfect to house such a complex. An alternative cinema (The Showcase) had opened up, so changing my plans from a multi-screen movie theatre to a plush live arts venue would no longer deny the people of Peterborough from seeing the latest Hollywood blockbuster.

I bought the old venue and soon went to work on turning it into a theatre fit for the West End. However, I did decide to siphon off a section of 15,000 square foot from the old building to be donated to the fledgling Peterborough University, to be used as its first location in the city. There was no fee involved – it was just a donation that I thought would help to improve Peterborough.

The renovation of the old cinema was to become my pet project. I decided to invest £9 million in the place – row after row of impeccable seats imported especially from the United States of America, luxurious carpets made in a bespoke fashion and state-of-the-art dressing rooms that could house the biggest names. I also decided to rename it 'The Broadway Theatre', to mark the fact it was now a live performance venue and not a cinema.

I didn't want to have the money sitting around in the bank, and I thought this would put it to good use. There needed to be a large place in Peterborough for the arts. I felt sure it would improve Peterborough as a city for years to come, and this belief was ratified when the *Peterborough Evening Telegraph* put the investment as their front page story… and then awarded me with its 'Pride Of Peterborough Person of the Year' award for 2001.

I suppose getting the football club promoted and investing all my money in Peterborough had caught their attention. The theatre opened for business with the usual thrust of excitement, including a visit from the senior civil servant for the Department of Culture, Media and Sport Philip Baker.

However, much like the Great Northern Hotel, interest again died down after the initial buzz. We would get spikes in attendance when big acts came to play, especially the top comedy talents such as Billy Connolly (who made packed crowds howl with laughter for successive nights... with many, including myself, being there for both evenings).

However, on most nights the attendances were poor. Some performances would go ahead despite only a handful of people sitting in the 1,200-seat auditorium, and more often than not they would cost us more to put on than we would recoup in sales.

However, I wasn't particularly worried about that. Just like PizzaExpress and Peterborough United had got off to a slow start, I was happy to stick with it. My desire for the perfect product and correct branding was more important to me than making a lot of cash. It seems strange to say, but I've never been in business to make money.

I took far greater pleasure sitting as one of half-a-dozen people enjoying a jazz concert in the theatre than when we would sell out to capacity for a lesser performance. On one occasion, I invited Dickie Bird up to see a performance by a highly rated Irish pop band called The Corrs, who were often at the top of the charts. It was a capacity crowd and when the band came out, I was surprised to see three strikingly beautiful women dressed seductively.

Then it dawned on me that 99 percent of the packed crowd was teenage boys. There was no denying The Corrs had musical talent, but the way they dressed and the wolf-whistles that emanated from the crowd left me furious. It felt like a peep show, not a concert.

I turned to Dickie, apologised and immediately stood to leave. On the way out, I spoke to one of the members of the booking committee and said I never wanted to see anything like that in my theatre again. Dickie looked shocked and said, "But Peter, the place is full. You'll make a packet."

The fact I courted my vision rather than large profits was nothing new. However, it was new that for the first time in decades, my incomings were lower than my shortcomings – and noticeably so.

What made this all the more worrying was that I had nothing to fall back on in terms of savings – it had all been invested in Peterborough. I had all my money tied up in various assets and my livelihood depended on them doing well. I had always been more 'asset rich' than 'cash rich', but I had now invested so much in the football club, theatre, restaurants and hotel that there just wasn't anything left in my savings.

43
HOW TO LOSE MILLIONS OF POUNDS… AND KEEP SMILING

While the £1 million per year I was spending on Peterborough United put the most significant steady dent on my wealth, there were other outgoings that also hit my wallet hard. I do not for one moment regret any of them – even though they meant I had gone from being a multi-millionaire to being somebody who was asset-rich but cash-poor.

A lot of people ask me, "How did you lose tens of millions of pounds?" – the question itself is misleading in two parts. Firstly, a lot of my 'wealth', as erroneously reported every year in the *Sunday Times* Rich List, was tied up in assets that never exclusively belonged to me. Secondly – and most importantly – the money that had actually left my bank account was not 'lost'.

The semantics of that word suggest that it was misplaced. It was voluntarily handed over to causes that could use the money far more constructively than Peter Boizot ever could. My money was made while committing myself to my work for life. That meant no wife and no children, no worry of who will inherit my money and therefore no real desire to keep my bank balance bloated in old age.

My biggest regret in life is not having any children, but that fact allowed me to distribute my money while I was still living to causes I loved, and therefore enabled me to enjoy watching them prosper. That is a lovely silver lining to the disappointment of never becoming a father.

As well as my investments into Peterborough businesses, I felt that my money could help those who needed it more through philanthropy. To this end, I set up the Peter Boizot Foundation. We asked any good cause who could benefit from money to knock on my figurative door. Within a year, that door would have needed a new buzzer, knocker and full-time bouncer.

That is not a gripe – the Peter Boizot Foundation was set up to redistribute my wealth to those who needed it. Hundreds of causes applied, and thousands of people benefited. However, such efforts meant that my savings took a battering for many successive years (which, in addition to my losses at the football club, theatre and hotel, meant that I fell off the *Sunday Times* Rich List rather quickly).

Here is a quick look at how much my Foundation gave away in five years;

1997-1998: £1.481 million
1998-1999: £1.760 million
1999-2000: £0.668 million
2000-2001: £1.158 million
2001-2002: £1.200 million

I will look in some detail at the next year, from April 2002 to March 2003. My accountant would tell you that I lost £934,500. However, I would prefer to say that I managed to find home for almost a million pounds in one extremely rewarding financial year.

How do you give away £934,500? Well some of the donations were large, and some were smaller gifts to causes and charities whose livelihood was hopefully made easier by my intervention.

Starting on the big scale, St Catharine's College got £350,000 for new artificial hockey pitches (meaning the team could play on perfect surfaces all year round) and Peterborough Cathedral's roof campaign got £270,000. The main beams and roof bosses of the tower dated back to the 14th century, and my donation to make them structurally sound coincided with a building programme which extended the East End of the church.

My beloved King's School also received £270,000, which was a one-off donation with no intention specified – I just wanted them to use it as they best deemed fit. If one cannot help the school that helped him earn his wealth, what is the point of accumulating money?

Other causes approached me once they heard of the Peter Boizot Foundation. I gave £21,000 to the Inter-Action Social Enterprise Trust Ltd, which was set up by my old Soho friend Ed Berman to help amateur dramatics thrive in the capital.

A friend who was an alumnus of the Uppingham School told me of their financial plight, so I wrote a cheque for £25,000. To be honest, I'm not too sure where the money went to, but they were most appreciative. West London Action For Children received £2,000 and there was £1,000 each for the Tonbridge New Memorial Trust and the Lewis Winstock Trust (a charity in Hertfordshire which gave education and training to young people).

These causes all looked forward, but there was also money earmarked to help protect the nation's heritage. Although I had no children, I was still desperately keen for future generations to enjoy the splendour of the past. I gave £3,000 to the Royal Academy of Art, £2,500 for the National Galleries of Scotland, £1,000 to the Fenland Archaeological Trust and £500 each for the Venice in Peril Fund and the Ely Cathedral Trust.

There was still some more money for Peterborough – £2,500 each for St Andrew's United Reform Church and Peterborough High School and £2,000 for the city's Princes Trust.

As you can imagine, that all soon added up. As a consequence, my accounts rarely did. My long-suffering accountant told me that in that year I had given away £528,000 in Peterborough and £406,500 elsewhere – and this was on top of the running costs of my various businesses.

I am still a comfortable man, but it is true that I am not as rich now as I once was. But I earned that money doing what I loved, and I suppose I lost it supporting what I loved. At the end of it all, the circular flow of money has spun around a full turn. The money may have been 'mine' for a few years, but I never felt true possession over it.

Money has no owner – only takers (and temporary custodians). I am overwhelmingly proud that I was able to redistribute that cash into causes that I felt deserved it.

So, no, I don't feel any financial regrets. People ask me if I was taken advantage of, as if my advancing years turned me from a business tycoon into a gibbering baboon within a few short months. Of course not – I made conscious decisions, supported by good people. And I would do it all again.

44
SELLING THE POSH

It was no secret that money had been haemorrhaging out of my bank account, and soon the offers started to come in for my businesses. In February 2002, a generous offer came in for Kettner's when PizzaExpress offered me £1.95 million – an acceptable price and a fitting owner, seeing as Kettner's had previously been an unofficial part of the PizzaExpress necklace.

I was strongly recommended by my financial advisers to accept it. However, the sale itself encountered something of a hiccup after a squabble over a rare painting of the chef who inspired the restaurant. PizzaExpress wanted to retain the image of Auguste Kettner, which hung pride of place in the main room, but I was adamant that I would not sell the painting – only the restaurant.

I planned to transport the painting of Monsieur Kettner up to Peterborough, where it could be displayed in the art gallery or on the walls of the Great Northern. In the end, a rather humorous deal was done. PizzaExpress said to me that if they could keep the painting, I would get a free glass of Dom Perignon champagne in Kettner's for the rest of my life.

I was sold – and so was the restaurant.

However, as well as raising money through that sale, I was strongly advised that I needed to stop losing so much money through the football club. At a cost of £1 million per year, Peterborough United were by far my most financially draining business.

I simply could no longer afford to keep pumping money into the Posh, and knew it was time to look for a change in my role. I felt I had achieved my ambition of making the club better off than when I took over, and put the club up for sale.

I hadn't publicly announced my ambition to sell the Posh – although my decision had been made, I wanted to do things properly and behind closed doors. I don't like to do my business deals in the public domain. As such, my plans to sell the club had not yet been revealed.

However, the sale of Kettner's led to hints that change was on the horizon at the football club. After the £2 million deal went through, a journalist from the *Peterborough Evening Telegraph* phoned me to congratulate me on the almost £2 million deal, and asked what I planned to do with the money. I explained that it would help my financially challenged projects in Peterborough, and he asked if that meant money for Peterborough United.

I answered his question honestly, and said I would not put any of the money into the football club.

You can imagine the outrage this caused! The paper ran with a story that implied the cash-strapped football club's owner had been given £2 million, but the old scrooge was refusing to hand it over.

Having already given millions of my own money to the cause, I was deeply saddened by the story and the furious reaction of the fans. But I bit my tongue and attempted to push the sale through behind closed doors.

In terms of the sale of the club, there were three options on the table. The worst was to call the administrators in – this would prompt a fire sale of players on the cheap and the loss of lots of the unsung heroes who worked tirelessly behind the scenes. The benefit would be that current director Alf Hand and I would still be creditors, and the administrators could help get our finances back on track.

Option two was to sell up to a consortium that, to be honest, I wasn't too sure about. They offered me a fair amount of money but I was warned that they saw the club as a gateway to a lucrative property deal. The ground had a huge retail value – especially as the city council eyed it as a prime sight for housing on the long-discussed South Bank River Nene redevelopment.

Credibility to this came from their offer of £135,000 to purchase the Moy's Road stand if I didn't decide to sell the club. This was a derisory amount, as access to that stand was extremely valuable and the land could be sold for millions. Rather than offering an alternative, this suggested to me that they were more interested in doing property deals than looking after the best interests of the club I loved.

Option three was to sell to a consortium headed by Alf, which if successful would make manager Barry Fry the chairman. They also had the backing of a millionaire named Colin Hill, but I believe he was to be a silent partner.

This was by far the worst for me financially. Whereas options one and two would see me recoup a chunk of the £7.5 million I had spent on the club, option three would see me get just £250,000. However, I am not greedy and had just pocketed £1.95 million from selling Kettner's, and there were numerous non-financial benefits that appealed to me. Most importantly – they were all people with Peterborough United in their veins, and I had no doubt that they simply wanted to do what was best for the only part of the club I cared about – what the starting eleven did on the pitch.

I tried to keep these dealings private, but in doing so started to gain more and more negative press and abuse from the crowds

I had spent all this money on stabilising the club when it was in its darkest hour in 1997. I had handed over £7.5 million of my own money, and now I was starting to become its biggest villain. Luckily, I have thick skin and was able to brush off their criticism as just the rough and tumble that came with football clubs.

I knew that even if the fans couldn't see it, the club was stronger now off and on the pitch than when I had joined. I had to sell, but I wanted to make sure that I sold to the best offer for Peterborough United (which was not necessarily the best offer for Peter Boizot). The idea was to create a strong club that could stand the test of time, and continue to entertain the people of Peterborough for years to come.

I invited Barry to discuss the options – although he was inextricably linked to Alf's bid, Barry was still a man who I trusted to tell it to me straight. First of all, Barry said to ignore the fans and the newspaper headlines. He said that both are short-term opinions that change by the week in football unlike in any other business.

However, he said both would be catastrophically worse if I sold to the administrators or the (alleged) property developers. The former would have broken the team up, and the latter could sell the stadium and make the club homeless.

Barry was quite adamant that pursuing either option would be the worst things to ever happen to the club, and would even make me an enemy of the Posh fans. He said they would come to the Great Northern and burn it down.

Therefore, these options were both unthinkable, and the complete opposite of my dream of creating a positive legacy in my hometown. I didn't want to wait around for another buyer, as I wanted to avoid the same fate that met the administration-plagued Queens Park Rangers during the same season. QPR entertained dozens of 'interested' parties that all turned out to be time wasters – I wanted to sell quickly.

There was only one option – to sell to Alf's consortium.

The deal went through fairly swiftly, and the new consortium appointed Barry as chairman as well as manager. After the deal was done, I had lost just over £7.5 million on the club.

I was given a complimentary season ticket in the directors' box and, a decade later, I am delighted that the club's future seems secure. They have recently jumped between the second and third tier of English football. Posh have a dynamic young chairman in Darragh MacAnthony and a team that boasts international footballers.

Darragh is an amazing man for numerous reasons, but not least because he is one of the youngest chairmen in the country after buying the club while in his mid-30s. I don't know Darragh well, but I wish him all the best – it's a demanding role, so maybe it's a good thing that a young man is at the helm. He also reminds me of myself – a workaholic who trusts his instincts and follows his passions.

The stadium has continued to cause problems long after I have left. Firstly there was an issue in which the football club was separate to the freehold (the stadium) and each were owned by different people in the consortium. This caused all sorts of headaches that I was pleased to be away from.

The council bought the ground in 2009, and ever since Darragh seems to be in a perpetual battled over the rates and the rent. It's a great shame that the club doesn't own its stadium, but that's none of my business now.

The fact that little old Posh are often competing in the second tier of English football is something that fills me with great pride. And although I enjoyed my time there, I'm happy to leave the headaches to Darragh and just enjoy the games as a fan.

Most rewarding of all is the fact that so many Posh fans' opinion of me couldn't be much higher. At every game, I am approached by strangers who say that if it wasn't for my intervention and stabilisation of the club, the Posh wouldn't be in anywhere near as good shape as they are now – financially sound, with a committed owner and a good team.

That I helped with that is a source of great pride.

45
BATTLING THE BANKS

After selling Posh and Kettner's, I was left with just over £2 million. This money helped me to continue running the other businesses for another couple of years, but sadly it just wasn't enough to sustain them without any help from the banks.

The problem with my business interests is that I'm a dreamer and an idealist – I'm not a man whose mind is governed by profit margins. Yet even if you have a good idea, bankers will tell you that you need money to run those businesses.

Just like back in 1965, when I would beg and plead with banks for favourable loans when starting PizzaExpress, I found myself with cap in hand speaking to lenders in my hometown. I knew full well that, if they were given the chance to bed-in, the theatre, hotel and restaurant would all be successful. However, bank managers in the 21st century were more interested with the projections on an Excel spreadsheet than the content of a salesman's pitch.

My pleas for loans were rejected. I still maintain that if I had even a few more thousand pounds, the businesses would have thrived. Far from being given any assistance from the banks, I was facing the financial abyss. My overdrafts were called in, meaning I had to pay off my debts or face bankruptcy. The irony that I could not get any financial help after years of donating millions of pounds per year to needy causes was not lost on me – but that's life.

As the banks wouldn't give me any money, I had no choice but to sell assets to the best bidder. I won't go into the deals in too much financial detail, but over the space of the next few years my empire crumbled faster than a sandcastle in a storm surge.

I approached the sales with a sense of positivity – just as I had left Posh in a better shape than I found them in, I was hopeful that with the right buyers all of my businesses could continue to serve Peterborough long after I had sold them.

The first in my chain to go was the Broadway Theatre. I had no choice but to accept a considerably smaller offer than I wanted from a Peterborough-based Italian businessman named Rinaldo Fasulo. The deal went through in August 2004. After buying it as a dilapidated cinema, I had turned it into a theatre with all the artistic potential in the world. I took great solace in the fact that, although I was no longer its owner, the £10 million I had invested in the theatre meant that Peterborough had a beautiful building that could host top-level performances.

Rinaldo also made an acceptable offer to take over Gaston's. It was a great shame to see it go, but again I had no choice in the matter and sold up.

I thought I was still a good owner, and testament to that was the fact that neither Gaston's nor the Broadway Theatre prospered after I sold them. They were both in perfect condition when the ownership changed, yet both seemed to struggle when I was no longer at the helm.

Despite these sales, my debts continued to grow and the banks still needed to be paid. I made it my number one priority to keep hold of the Great Northern Hotel(and the adjoining Guildenburgh Art Gallery). In another bid to raise some cash, I sold another asset in Pizza On The Park in 2006. Like Kettner's, it was bought by my old company, PizzaExpress Ltd.

Sadly, it also struggled after I handed over the deeds. Within three years of me selling up, the former jewel in London's live music scene was also no more. A most perplexing planning decision saw the City of Westminster take away its historic basement room because of a regulation which stated the basement could not house music. Nearby groups such as the Knightsbridge Association, the Belgravia Residents Association and the Royal Parks agreed with the council's decision, and so that magnificent jazz venue tragically died.

Yet again though, this sale did not solve my ongoing cash flow problems. I struggled on for another couple of years but, in April 2009, I was finally forced to sell the hotel and gallery. Insurmountable debts continued to mount up and, to my disappointment, administrators from Tenon Recovery were ultimately appointed. They quickly found a buyer – something that was not surprising, due to the hotel's fine upkeep and prominent location.

I was crestfallen to be forced to lose the hotel – the last of my Peterborough businesses. I moved all of my things out of the hotel and into my new house. Gratefully, before being forced out I found a home on the delightful surroundings of the Cathedral Precincts, and I was always treated magnificently by those people at the cathedral who remained forever grateful to me for the donations I had made.

I left the Great Northern Hotel in an impeccable condition for the owners, and just like with the Broadway Theatre, Gaston's and Pizza On The Park, I hoped it would flourish after I had left. After all, my plan was to create a long-lasting legacy for my hometown – now it was time for the new owners to take on the baton.

Days after I had sold the hotel, I came back to collect my treasured eight-foot statue of Duke Ellington from my mother's memorial garden. I would have happily left it if I knew it would go to good use, but I understood the new owners planned to demolish the garden to create a bigger car park.

It's not for me to tell others how to run their business, but this seemed a terrible shame – not just to my mother's memory, but also to the many people who would no longer be able to have christening and wedding parties in the garden. I was baffled with how it fitted into the owners' idea of an upmarket boutique hotel, and my criticism was matched by the shocked chairman of the Peterborough Civic Society, Peter Lee.

However, the story did not end there. When I went to collect my statue, the space where it had stood so proudly as a symbol to inspire the city of Peterborough was now empty. I was furious. Where was this £40,000 statue that I had commissioned, transported and put in the hotel's grounds?

I immediately phoned the police to report it as stolen. However, when they took my statement they seemed uninterested. A report came back that said the statue belonged to the hotel, which no longer belonged to me. I contacted the hotel's new owners, but they were not interested in reporting it as stolen.

I have never laid eyes on that statue again – a symbol bought simply to inspire others has seemingly either been hidden away in storage, or has been melted down and sold on as jewellery. That thought disappointed me more than the loss of any of my businesses. I have my theories on where the statue has gone, but I am not one for dragging anybody's name through the mud. All I will say is that if the person or people responsible have it hidden away somewhere, I would appreciate if they were to return it to me so I could put it back on public display – no questions asked.

I try not to ruminate on negative thoughts. Sitting in my new flat on the grounds of Peterborough Cathedral, I had plenty of time to consider what had happened since 1993, and how I had gone from having £35 million in the bank to investing it all into a new empire for my hometown – an empire that was then taken away from me.

People often ask me whether I regret my business decisions, and my answer is always the same; absolutely not.

All I ever wanted to do was give back to Peterborough, and I had succeeded in doing that because everything I touched entertained people and thrust new life into the city.

This belief was gratefully re-enforced when an unexpected letter came through my new flat's letter-box one morning. I may not have been sitting in as grandiose a home as I had enjoyed when living at the Great Northern or Lowndes Square in London, but the contents of this letter filled me with far greater pride than four walls and a roof ever could.

It was from Peterborough City Council, and it invited me to attend a ceremony where they were going to grant me the Freedom of the City of Peterborough. Although being awarded Freedom of the City does not carry any rights or responsibilities, it is the highest symbolic honour for any citizen. It is a symbol of appreciation for your work.

While I never did anything in Peterborough for fame or recognition, to be made a Freeman of my hometown showed that, despite the way some of the businesses ended, it had all been worth it.

The ceremony saw me lead a procession through the city centre. While I walked through the streets of the city I had helped to rejuvenate, I waved at the crowds who had gathered to watch. With a gleam in my eye, memories of the decades that had led to this moment rushed before my eyes.

A naïve, wide-eyed teenage trip to Italy made me fall in love with pizza, and my love of that food granted me riches of which I had never dreamed. In turn, that money helped me to improve Peterborough, whose people appreciated my efforts so much that I was given the freedom of my hometown.

What a wonderful end to a wonderful story!

Photo by Ben Davis

46
CARRY ON CARRYING ON

At the time of writing, I am 84 years of age. I have my good days and my bad days – the ratio seems to fluctuate erratically regardless of what pills my doctors ask me to throw down my throat. My memory sometimes lets me down – it tends to be better in the morning than night, and often I wake up instantly remembering the things that I spent hours trying to recall the previous evening.

I still hold the position of 'president' of PizzaExpress to this day, which grants me more symbolic power than real responsibilities. I am delighted to see the company thriving with over 6,000 employees and a £100 million plus valuation. Not bad for a restaurant started up without a business plan!

After I stepped aside at PizzaExpress, a branch finally opened in my hometown. Despite my fears, the local Italians had nothing but praise for it! You can see me in there three or four times a week, often sitting under a fabulous painting of myself that hangs on the wall.

I still live in Peterborough, in a flat that I jokingly describe as my bachelor's pad in the luxurious west end of the city. Many people recognise me in the streets and football stands, but with each year my fame seems to diminish slightly. I notice this most in Peterborough's PizzaExpress, where more and more people seem to ask me why a portrait of me is hanging on the wall.

The businesses I tried to help in Peterborough have enjoyed various degrees of success since I was forced to sell them. The hotel is still in good stead and the football club is in much better shape than before I took over. However, Gaston's has now closed down and the Broadway Theatre, which could host a top show at the drop of a hat, has endured many years of dormancy.

Permanently reopening the theatre has become my latest crusade. If the right shows were put on, the seats would be filled – as was shown by a successful short run of performances put on by leading West End theatre producer Bill Kenwright in the winter of 2013. Yet the run was over all too quickly, and the building closed once again. I can't reopen it on my own because I don't have the same fortunes now as I did when I bought it in 2001. But that hasn't stopped me approaching banks for loans, or appealing for partners to join me in a consortium. Sadly those pleas have thus far fallen on deaf ears, but I still battle on and hope to attend many more shows in the theatre.

I sometimes fear that my dream of making Peterborough come to life is analogous to that of the hunter's desire to catch the white whale in Moby Dick. The hunter and I will both forever chase that dream, but it may never quite be realised.

Yet I have not given up on my hometown. I never will. I still think it has great potential, and recently set up the semi-eponymous PeterBorough Club in a bid to promote social activity around the city. I am also toying with the idea of setting up a new vegetarian restaurant called Peter's Place.

Just like there was a lack of pizza restaurants in 1965, I think there is a huge gap in the market for a top class vegetarian chain. I may now be an octogenarian – but what is stopping me from filling that gap? As I often tell those around me, there is nothing to do but carry on carrying on.

My sister Wendy has often claimed that 'Peter Boizot doesn't stop until Peter Boizot gets what Peter Boizot wants' – and she is quite right. Even if everything around me was going wrong, I would rather climb a tree and say it's going well than stay on the ground and admit there are problems. That's just the way I am wired. That sheer bloody-mindedness led to my improbable prosperity – and also meant that my fortune only had a temporary tenure.

Most importantly, I will always be proud that at every stage of my life I have invested everything into the things I love – whether it was pizza, jazz, heritage, sport or the arts. I think my work has benefited all of my passions, which is a fine footprint to leave behind.

Challenges have been constant throughout my life, but I think that my experiences show that any test can be turned into a success. Prosperity is available to all – especially those who shun the traditional definition of 'work' in favour of pursuing their passions.

I hope this book will inspire you to commit your life to what you love.

Ron Simson

I mention Ron Simon a number of times in my book.

I am sorry to tell you that my dear friend Ron has passed away.

I am sure he would have been pleased to read this book, which he was so helpful in putting together.